The Way I Remember It

World War Two

By

George A. Flynn

ISBN: 1-4033-9500-4 (e-book)
ISBN: 1-4033-9501-2 (Paperback)
ISBN: 1-4033-9502-0 (Dustjacket)

Library of Congress Control Number: 2002095790

This book is printed on acid free paper.

Printed in the United States of America
Bloomington, IN

1stBooks – rev. 11/13/02

I must acknowledge that this book would never have been written if it were not for the urging of my beautiful wife, Virginia. She told me that my war experiences should be told to future generations.

TABLE OF CONTENTS

CHAPTER ONE:

DON'T WORRY MOM I'LL BE BACK

Ever since the war ended, deep down in the back of my mind, I figured, that someday I should write about my World War Two experiences, which were numerous.

They say better late than never. I hope that applies to me, because I am starting to write today, which is Tuesday, February 22, 1996, which is over Fifty Years since my days as a soldier. I am now Seventy Four years old. But I figure, it is slightly possible, that I may not live forever, and should I die without this writing, all present and future members of my family would be deprived of a very interesting account of my World War Two experiences, which were scary, exciting, and most unpredictable, not only from day to day, but also from hour to hour. It could also be said from minute to minute. There were also humorous and very pleasant experiences.

I have Japan to thank for making me a soldier because the Japanese bombed Pearl Harbor in Hawaii on December 7, 1941, which was a big U.S. Naval base. It was a surprise attack, we were not at war with Japan, in fact, at that time, we were not at war with anybody. As a matter of fact, Japan at

1

that time had their ambassadors in Washington D.C. talking with our government about signing some sort of agreement stating we would never make war on each other. While they were in Washington talking peace, their Navy with airplane carriers were on their way to bomb Pearl Harbor. If that isn't a sneak maneuver, I never heard of one.

Well, as a result of Japan's sneak attack, they sank and destroyed many of our Naval ships. Also, many of our soldiers, sailors, marines, nurses, doctors, and civilians were killed or wounded.

As a result, President Roosevelt, of the United States, declared war on Japan.

A day or so later, Germany declared war on us, because we declared war on Japan, and Germany, Japan and Italy, were called the Axis powers, and they had all previously signed a pact stating, if one country was attacked, the others had to help. So when they declared war on us, we declared war on them, meaning Germany and Italy.

Roughly, the way it went, the enemy was Japan, Germany and Italy, and on our side were, United States, England, Canada, Russia, Australia, and New Zealand.

So where do I fit into all this? It goes sort of like this. At age Twenty, I was drafted into the Army on November 10, 1942. Before I was honorably discharged from the Army on October 21, 1945, a hell of a lot of things happened.

The 16th Infantry Regiment of the First Infantry Division, fought through eight Major campaigns, in World War Two. And I, as a first aid man with the 16th Infantry Regiment of the First Infantry Division, I fought through seven of those eight Major Campaigns.

I saw action in Africa, Sicily, France, Belgium, Germany, and Czechoslovakia. I made two D-Day invasions with the 16th Infantry Regiment of the First Infantry Division. I made the D-Day invasion in Sicily, and the D-Day invasion in Normandy, France.

Well to start at the beginning. I was drafted into the Army on November 10, 1942, and sent to Camp Pickett in Virginia. They put me in the Medics, and I didn't like that, so I asked to see the Company Commander.

I told him I didn't want to be a Medic. I told him I wanted to be a rifleman with the Infantry. He told me, the only way I could get out of being a medic, was to volunteer to become a paratrooper, and I said okay. He then said first I would have to do two things. Number one, I would have to pass a very strict physical examination, and if I passed the physical, next I would have to take a special obstacle course training program. He then said, if I passed both, he would then sign the papers, and send me to Fort

3

Benning, Georgia, to Paratrooper Training school. I said "Okay." I figured anything is better than being a medic, even jumping out of airplanes. I didn't tell him I was allergic to height. I figured when it's time to jump, I will just close my eyes and jump. Also, I was never in an airplane, I figured that would be an exciting experience. So he scheduled the physical examination, which I passed. Then for the next few days, I took the special obstacle training course, which I also passed.

Then it was set up for me to leave Camp Pickett on a Monday morning, for my trip to Georgia. But Friday night, which would be my last Friday as a medic, I went with a few friends to celebrate at the P.X. We all had a few beers. After a few hours at the P.X., I started to feel sick, I got the chills and started to perspire. So I left the P.X. and went back to the barracks and went right to bed. When the Officer, who was a Doctor, went through the barracks, taking bed check, to make sure nobody was absent, one of my friends told the Officer, that I didn't look good, and I had the chills. The Doctor took my temperature. He said I had a 104 degree temperature. He then called for an ambulance and sent me to the base hospital.

Monday morning, I told the nurse I wanted to leave the hospital, so I could join the paratroopers. She said "No way," I still had a very high temperature, so they kept me in the hospital about two weeks.

4

When I got out of the hospital, I asked the Company Commander if I could be sent to Fort Benning Georgia, to join the paratroopers. He said I would have to wait for the next group, in about two or three weeks.

But before I was called for the paratroopers, I was sent to Fort Mead, Maryland, to prepare, to be sent overseas. We were given different inoculations and such. I think I stayed there about a week. From there I was sent to Fort Slocum, New York, which is on a small island on Long Island Sound, just off New Rochelle, New York. I stayed there for about a month.

One day, we were put on what resembled a big river boat, and sent to a pier in Brooklyn. We got off the riverboat and got right onto a waiting troop transport ship and we sailed that same night. They wouldn't tell us where we were going. Most of us were raw recruits, just out of basic training. We were a mixed group, most were infantry, some were artillery and some were medics, like me and various others.

At this time, the German Submarines were sinking a lot of American ships, up and down the American East Coast. Therefore, our ship left Brooklyn after dark, and we headed right out into the Atlantic Ocean. At dawn, we saw that we were in a small convoy. The next day or so, we seemed to circle around, and change course a lot, I guess, trying to avoid the German Submarines. Each day, more ships would come out and join the convoy. We had all kinds of ships in the convoy. Troop Ships, cargo ships and a lot of Navy ships for protection. In all our zig-zagging, we must have sailed pretty far South because the weather seemed nice and warm for a few days. One day the Navy Destroyers started zipping around, in and out of the convoy. After a while, they dropped some depth charges. We don't know if they hit any German submarines. We just kept zig-zagging and kept going. I'll tell you one thing, from then on, it wasn't a nice feeling, realizing that at any moment our ship could be blown to Hell. A day or so later, at night, we sailed through the Straight of Gibralter. We were now in the Mediterranean Sea. We kept changing course in the Mediterranean Sea. Again, I suppose to avoid German submarines.

CHAPTER TWO:

AFRICA

About a day or so later, we headed South towards Africa. We were then told that we are going to land in Oran, North Africa. On the way into the harbor, we passed a lot of half-sunken ships. Most of them were in shallow water, close to shore. They looked as if they had been damaged by bombs or artillery, and set on fire. When we docked in Oran, we were quickly loaded into Army trucks and taken away. We rode about forty minutes to an Army replacement center. All we could see was big Army tents. It was near the town of Arzue, near the Mediterranean Sea. I stayed about two weeks in the replacement center. Everyday we would have to line up and do exercises, push ups, deep knee bends, and such. It was to keep us physically fit. We would also go on marches, and run up and down big hills. They would have a bunch of roll calls all day long. When your name was called, they would load you on a truck, when the truck was full, the truck would leave camp and take you someplace, where you would join a regular division, as a replacement, for somebody who was killed or wounded.

George A. Flynn

One day a few of us hitched a ride to Oran, for a couple of beers, and to see what the town looked like. It was late at night when we got back to the replacement camp. The next morning I was told to report to the First Sergeant, which I did. He asked where I was yesterday; so I told him. He laughed and said, "Boy, you really screwed up" and said they called my name yesterday to ship out. He said they needed a bunch of men to work in the Army Post Office in Oran, and I was on the list to go there, so they sent somebody else to take my place. He said, "Do you know what that means?" I said, "No." He said I would have probably spent the entire war working in the Army Post Office in Oran. He said, "Now there is no telling where you will be sent." I said, "I guess you're right Sergeant, I really did screw up." He said, "Get the hell out of here," which I did.

When I got back to my tent, I told the other soldiers what the Sergeant said. They said my name was called a couple of times yesterday, I figured oh well, you win some you lose some. In the next two and a half years, I realized what a mistake I made. A few days later, my name was called again. This time I was sent to Tunisia to join the 16th Infantry Regiment of the First Infantry Division, still as a medic. So I spent the remainder of the war as a first aid man, with the Big Red One.

When my name was called this time in the replacement center near Oran, I was told to hop on a truck with a bunch of other soldiers. We were in a small truck convoy. They told us we were heading to the front lines somewhere in Tunisia. We rode for a couple of days. Then one evening, we pulled into a big field where there were a few very big tents, with big white boxes, with big red crosses painted all over the tents. We were told it was an Army Field Hospital to take care of the wounded. We could hear artillery shells being fired and exploding in the not too far distance. The next morning, about three or four ambulances pulled up. We were told to get into the ambulance. There were about five of us in the ambulance that I got into. Most of them had rifles, I had a red cross strapped to my arm. I asked the soldiers with the rifles, if they would like to change the rifle for my red cross, they laughed and said "No thanks". If I had a choice, I would have gladly swapped the red cross for a rifle, but I guess it just wasn't meant to be. We rode for about an hour. When the ambulance stopped, somebody from outside the ambulance opened the door. It was a Corporal, who told us to hurry and get off, which we did. I looked around and saw a bunch of army mattress covers lying on the ground. They were all loaded with something. As soon as we got off the ambulance, they started loading the mattress covers into the ambulances. I asked what was in the mattress covers. They told me there was a body in each mattress cover. They were First Division soldiers, who were killed last night. There must have been about eight or ten bodies. As soon as the bodies were loaded, the

9

ambulances left. Then I looked around to see what was going on. We were on the side of a big hill, sort of like a mountain. The hill was covered with newly dug fox holes. Soldiers were still digging their fox holes. Some were sitting on the side of the fox holes, with their feet dangling into the fox holes. Some were sitting on the ground talking. Then a Staff Sergeant called us. He took our names, and then told us what to do, and where to go. He told me I would be a litter bearer. He told me to find an empty fox hole, and if I couldn't find one, to dig one. He said the deeper the better. So I looked around and found an empty one. I sat down on the edge of the fox hole admiring it, when a soldier tapped me on the shoulder and said, "I dug that hole, go dig your own." He was a rough, tired, dirty looking soldier. So I shut up, and started to dig my own fox hole. While digging I heard a commotion over by the small First Aid tent. I stopped digging and walked over to the First Aid tent to see what was going on. There was this soldier, walking up and down. He was sort of half crying and kept waving his hands and sort of shouting, but in a low voice. He said something like "Why don't they stop shooting? Why don't they stop shooting?" He said "I can't stand it." He kept repeating the same thing and kept walking up and down and around a small circle. I asked some of the medics, what his problem was. They told me that he seemed to have a mild case of Combat Fatigue. I don't remember if they evacuated him, or if they were able to quiet him down, because I went back to digging my fox hole. But I will say this, I saw him in Sicily and all the other campaigns after Africa. As far as I know, he was perfectly all right and never had another breakdown, after that one incident. As a matter of fact, he turned out to be a very brave, and well liked soldier.

The way one will act in combat, is very unpredictable. One day nothing bothers you, and you are considered a hero. The next day everything bothers you, and you are considered a coward. But the following day you could be back to being a hero again.

Just as I finished my fox hole, the Sergeant said, "Pack up, we are moving out." So I put my pack on and followed. We went about a quarter of a mile to another hill. The Sergeant said, "Okay - dig in." So I dug my second fox hole, on my first day. That's about the way it went with digging fox holes. In the months and years to follow, sometimes I dug three or four fox holes in a day or a night. Oh yes, there was some more digging, when you had to go to the toilet, that consisted of digging a small hole in the ground, and when finished you had to put the dirt back in the hole. If you didn't have diarrhea it wasn't too much digging. But if you had diarrhea, that could add up to quite a bit of digging also. When the war ended, and people asked me how I ever survived seven campaigns, I told them, "Because I had a guardian angel that never slept, and also, because I became a champion digger."

George A. Flynn

The next day Staff Sergeant Tim Lombard told me and another private Bill Summer, who I think got off the ambulance with me yesterday, also as a replacement, to take a litter and follow him, which I did. We went up another hill and crossed a road. On the side of the road was a newly dug small German soldiers' cemetery, about twelve graves with white crosses marking each grave. I was standing there, looking at the crosses, when the Sergeant told me to hurry and follow him. We went into a flat field, with a small, long hill on each side. There was an American half-track, that had hit a land mine, on the side of the field. There were a bunch of American Infantry soldiers all over the field. All of a sudden I heard some kind of a weird whistling sound. It sounded like it was getting closer and louder. I didn't know what it was. But all the Infantry soldiers around me hit the dirt. So I did the same thing. And just in time, because as I hit the ground, I heard a few very loud explosions. After a while as more shells were exploding, I heard a loud thump near my head. I looked to see what made the thump. About a foot and a half away from my head, I saw a large piece of jagged shiny metal about the size of my mess kit, stuck into the ground. I reached my hand out to touch it, but that turned out to be a mistake. When I touched it, I burnt my hand. There was a rifleman lying on the ground near me. I asked him what that hell the thing was? He laughed and said that it was part of the shell that just exploded over our heads. He said it was an air burst that exploded near the half-track. I said, "Oh, thanks and good bye." He said, "Where are you going?" I said "I am going to crawl as far as possible away from the half-track." He said "Good idea." We both crawled about fifty feet away. All of a sudden some more shells came in and these didn't explode in the air, these hit the ground, and then exploded. Some of them kicked rocks and dirt all over me. At that time I said some prayers. "If God wanted me, to take me now. I told him, if he didn't take me, that I wasn't going to mend my ways. I told him, I would still drink beer, and fool around with the girls."

So maybe drinking beer and fooling around with the girls isn't too bad, because he didn't take me. I also figured better to get killed on my second day of combat than the last day of the war. I also figured, if I got killed, my mother would be the richest mother in Bayside West. Because, when you went into the Army, they gave you a ten thousand dollar insurance policy. I don't think my mother even had more than one thousand dollars at the same time. My mother wins and I win, nobody loses. But I then thought, and I added, "God if you want me, kill me now, and take me. But please don't send me home a cripple. I don't want anybody to have to take care of me, and I don't want to have to depend on anybody."

So the way it turned out, I think he is a very good and understanding God, and I love him.

George A. Flynn

After the shelling stopped, the Sergeant said "Okay, let's go." So I followed him again. He went to the end of the small long hill on our left. There was a big boulder there. He stood on our side of the boulder. He then said to me and the other Private, who was also carrying a litter, "Now look out there. See this big open field in front of us?" I said "Yes." He then said "Look way out there, see that big hill at the end of the open field?" I said, "Yes." The hill was about a quarter of a mile away. He said, "One of our Infantry companies is on that hill. There are two wounded men there who must be evacuated by stretcher. They are badly wounded, and can't walk." He said, "Oh, one more thing. There is another long low hill on the left, as you step out from behind this boulder. The German Infantry is dug in on that hill. Every time somebody goes past this big boulder, a German machine gunner shoots at them." So the Sergeant said, "What I want you two guys to do is, each one of you take a litter and run as fast as you can to get the wounded." I said, "Sergeant there is no way I can out run a machine gun bullet. So what I would like to do is put my red cross patch up high on my left arm and carry the stretcher with my right hand over my right shoulder and then I would like to walk out from this big boulder real slow, and if he doesn't shoot, I would like to continue walking real slow. I don't intend to run. I think the slower I walk the better. I also don't intend to look to my left, where the German Infantry is dug in. I will just look straight

14

ahead towards our Infantry. That is what I would like to do, that is, if my plan is okay - with you." The Sergeant shook his head and laughed and said, "I don't care how you do it, so long as you get the wounded and bring them back." Then he looked at Private Summer and said, "What would you like to do, run or walk?" Summer said, "I think we would have a better chance walking." The Sergeant said okay -- good luck. So we both walked out real slow, each carrying a stretcher. Neither of us looked to the left, we just looked straight ahead, and walked one behind the other, real slow. Not a shot was fired. As we got close to our Infantry, I could see sort of a big cave opening, up on the side of the hill. And there were a lot of American Infantry soldiers all around there. As we got closer a few of them started hollering for us to run. But we didn't run, we just kept walking nice and slow. We got to our Infantry, without a shot being fired. Our guys were glad to see us, they said anytime they tried to go out in the field, they got shot at.

The Lieutenant said, "Okay - we have two badly wounded men here. They will have to be taken back on the stretchers." He said "I think it better if you evacuate them on one trip." So he said, "I will send two of my riflemen to help you carry the stretchers." He asked for volunteers. So two riflemen volunteered. Then I said "Wait a minute, I want to take my red cross, off my left shoulder, and put it on my right shoulder so the German

Soldiers can see it." The Lieutenant said that was a good idea. I then said "I still think we should walk nice and slow going back. When they see us carrying the wounded maybe they will let us go through without shooting at us." We all agreed. So we started out real slow again. I was first out, so they could see my red cross. I carried the front end of the stretcher, and the rifleman with his rifle over his shoulder carried the rear of the stretcher. Nothing happened, so Private Summer with his red cross on his right shoulder came out carrying the front of his stretcher, and the rifleman with his rifle over his shoulder carried the rear of the stretcher. We carried the wounded all the way back, and not one shot was fired.

At this time I would like to say the German Army fighting in Africa were all regular Army career soldiers and they obeyed the Geneva Conference, who wrote the rules of war. That is the reason myself and Private Summer didn't get killed that day. They saw my Red Cross, and the rule book says don't shoot a medic. That's what I was counting on when I told the Sergeant, I would rather walk through the open field to get the wounded, instead of running.

At this point, I would like to thank every German Infantry Soldier who was dug in on that hill that day. Especially the machine gunner. If we ever meet, the Schnapps is on me.

When we got out of the line of fire that day, I think we all took a deep breath, and thanked the Good Lord. We then carried the wounded about another quarter of a mile, down the hill to the First Aid station, where the doctors were waiting to give them blood plasma, perform emergency operations, remove shrapnel, bullets, or what have you. When the ambulance came, they were taken to a field hospital. When we arrived at the First Aid Station, carrying the two wounded, the two riflemen who helped us carry the litters, said "so long," and they both went back up the hill to rejoin their rifle company. Later I heard that when the first one stepped out from behind the big boulder, he got about fifty feet into the big open field, and he was shot.

The next few days, nothing too exciting happened. Then one night about 10:00 PM, they told us to pack up, "We are moving up." I was assigned to carry one end of the litter and on the stretcher was a very big medical chest, it was about two feet, by two feet by three feet. Maybe even bigger. It was very heavy. The Sergeant told us not to talk, not to smoke, and not to make any noise. He said, "We are going single file, and to leave about ten yards space between us and the man in front of us." He said, "Whatever you do, don't let the man in front of us, get out of sight." He said, "If we get lost, we are on our own, nobody will come looking for us." He also said, "We will be sort of going through the German lines and we are

17

not sure where the Germans are, and he hopes they don't know where we are." He said, "Don't dare make a sound and don't dare stop. Be sure to keep up." I would be willing to bet that whoever was leading the column, wasn't carrying a stretcher with a big heavy medical chest on it. We practically had to trot to keep up. After awhile, I was thinking of making some noise, so the Germans would shoot me and get this silliness over with. But being a good First Division soldier, I didn't make any noise. I just cursed a little and kept going, like the rest of the miserable bastards. I figured if they can do it, so can I. We must have gone at least five miles, maybe longer. We were going mostly in low rocky land like dried out streams. We kept slipping and falling on loose rocks. Carrying the front of the stretcher you could see your footing, but carrying the rear of the stretcher all you could see was the stretcher. You couldn't see what you were stepping on, so we took turns carrying the front and back. Finally the Sergeant said, "This is it, dig in. We will stay the night here." Nobody argued. Everybody dug a fox hole and went to sleep, except those on guard duty. When I woke up in the morning, there were two little things that looked like baby lobsters in the fox hole with me. They told me they were scorpions. So I figured I am learning something new every day.

Around noon time I spotted a big puddle down at the bottom of the hill. It had water running in on one side, and out the other side. I asked the

Sergeant if we could drink the water? He said, "No, the Germans may have poisoned the water." So I said, "If nobody is going to drink the water, will it be all right if I take a bath in it?" He looked at me as if I was crazy. He laughed again and said "Okay, go ahead." So I went down the hill, got undressed, and walked into the middle of the puddle. It was about two feet deep and about twenty feet in diameter. I took a bath, and felt like a million dollars. Not that I know what a million dollars feels like. By the time I got dressed, there must have been about ten more soldiers in the same puddle, taking baths. By the time it got dark, I think about two hundred soldiers took a bath there. Next day, we were still there, and soldiers were still taking baths.

The next day we moved about a half mile or so, and dug more fox holes but no place to take a bath at this location. The Sergeant told two of us to each take a litter and follow him. There were big hills and valleys all over the place. There was a road going in and between the hills. We could hear tanks coming up the road. I asked if they were German tanks or our tanks? He said, "I don't know, but keep down and don't let them see you." I kept down, but I kept peeking. He finally said that they were American tanks. There were three of them. They pulled off the road, and stopped behind a big hill, like a mountain. Some Infantry soldiers were talking and pointing things out to the guys in the tanks. After a while, one of the tanks came out from behind the hill and started towards a hill in the distance. He went about five hundred yards, and he was knocked out. After awhile the second tank came out from behind the hill and started to go the same way the first tank went but he only got about half way there, and he also got knocked out. After awhile the third tank turned around and went back where he came from. Later we found out that there was a German tank dug in on the side of the mountain. The guys in our tanks couldn't even see the German tank, because it was dug in and camouflaged. It's a good thing they didn't sent the third tank in. The way I understood it, the First Division Infantry assaulted and took the hill that night.

All told in Africa, I saw very little action. I think only about two weeks on the front lines until the German Army surrendered on May 13, 1943.

Over the next two years, I became very friendly with many First Division soldiers who went through all eight campaigns. I only went through seven campaigns, but they told me about the big major battles that I missed. And I thanked the Good Lord that I missed them. The First Division made the D-Day landing in North Africa on the beaches of Arzue. Their main objective was the town of Oran, which was a seaport town which was badly needed for the North African campaign to be a success. When the First Infantry Division landed at Arzue, there was a French Garrison there. So the First Division had to fight the French soldiers for a few hours, until the French Garrison surrendered. From Arzue they pushed on to take the town of Oran, which was also defended by French soldiers. Now with Oran in American hands, the Allies had a major seaport, to bring in supplies, such as tanks, artillery, ammunition, more combat divisions, replacements, food and medical supplies. So that was one big battle I am glad I missed.

Next the Battle of Kassarine Pass, which was a very severe battle with numerous German tanks and Infantry.

After Kassarine Pass, was the Battle of El Guettar. As a result of these three major battles, the First Division suffered numerous casualties. That's probably why I went to the First Division instead of the Post Office in Oran. But such was life during World War Two.

The First Division had to fight the French, Italian and German armies before the war ended.

After the Germans surrendered in Africa, we went back near the Oran area, and set up camp. We slept out in pup tents and such, out in wooded areas so the German planes couldn't see us if they flew over.

On the way back from Tunisia, we came back in a truck convoy. As we passed through different towns, all the people were waving and smiling at us. On the way back, one day the convoy stopped along the side of the road. I think it was just outside the town of Consentine. It was a beautiful place. Big trees on both sides of the road that made it look as if you were in a tunnel. There was a deep ditch on the side of the road, which must have been about a half a mile long. The ditch was full of about two feet of clear running water. The convoy stopped and the Officers said we would be here for awhile. If we wanted to take baths in the ditch, it was okay. The convoy stopped on the right side of the road, and the ditch was on the left side of the road. We were all dirty and sweaty. In about two minutes, every soldier and officer and all, were standing naked in the ditch taking a bath. The convoy must have been about a half mile long and every soldier was in the ditch. Then the funniest thing happened. All of a sudden at one end of the convoy, all the soldiers started hollering, laughing, shouting and whistling. We could see a jeep convoy coming down the road. At first we didn't know what was going on. But as the jeep convoy which was going slow, neared us, we could see what was going on. So we all started hollering, laughing, and whistling because it was a convoy of about twenty jeeps, and in each jeep there were about four American Army nurses. So we all jumped out of the ditch completely naked, waving at the nurses. We invited them in but they just laughed and kept driving. One of our soldiers said, "So that's what an American girl looks like." I told the soldier next to me, too bad it wasn't the nurses in the ditch bathing, and us driving by. He agreed that would have been much better.

We went to a wooded area near Oran and set up camp. About a week later, I got dysentery and was sent to a hospital in Oran. They kept me in the hospital about two weeks. When I got out of the hospital, they told me that the First Division had moved out, and went to Algiers. They told me I had a choice, either I could hitch a ride to Algiers, or they would send me to a replacement center, but no guarantee that I would be sent back to the First Division. So I figured they were a jolly lot. So I told them I would prefer rejoining the First Division and they sent me to an Army Supply Depot. When there I reported to the office and told the Lieutenant my story. He said okay, there is a supply truck convoy leaving in about an hour for Algiers. When I arrived in Algiers, I retold my story and they sent me in a jeep to rejoin the First Division.

Back home at last, I figured, so I rejoined the Medical Detachment 16th Infantry of the First Division. I met some of my old friends, and asked what was cooking. They told me I should have gone to the replacement Depot. Because rumor had it, in a few days we were supposed to load on ships again and make another invasion. Rumor was correct. In about a week or so, we were taken to Algiers Harbor, and loaded aboard a Navy landing craft.

At this point I would like to tell you about a Captain O'Brien of Cannon Company 16th Infantry of the First Division. He was a very well liked, brave and a most interesting person. He was a West Point graduate. At this time, he had about fifteen years in the Army. He was Company Commander of Cannon Company. The reason I know about Captain O'Brien is, after two weeks into the Sicilian campaign, I was promoted from being a litter bearer to being a First Aid man with Cannon Company. Now Captain O'Brien was known for his pep talks and very interesting speeches. I didn't hear Captain O'Brien make this speech, but I was told all about it. Cannon Company was lined up on the dock in Algiers waiting to board the Navy landing craft for the Sicilian invasion. Captain O'Brien was walking up and down on the dock inspecting his troops, when all of a sudden he stopped and said "Sergeant Jayson, you are out of uniform. You don't have your leggings on. You are a disgrace to the American Army. You don't deserve the privilege of making another invasion with the First Division. Report to the kitchen crew, you will come in with them." And that is what I was told happened. After that, whenever a big battle was looming, the soldiers would tell the Sergeant "I lost my leggings." It became a standard joke in Cannon Company for the remainder of the war. There will be more about Captain O'Brien later on. I will say this much now, it was a very sad day in Cannon Company when Captain O'Brien was killed in action in Germany. It was like losing a father.

CHAPTER THREE:

SICILY

Now back in Algiers harbor around July 8, 1943; I was loaded onto a Navy ship. I think it was called the Chase. It wasn't a landing craft. It was a bigger ship. At that time I was still a litter bearer attached to the Third Battalion 16th Infantry, First Aid Station. We pulled out of the harbor that same night. For a day or so, we sailed East and West on the Mediterranean Sea I suppose, to confuse the Germans as to where we would land. Then all of a sudden, we could see land, off to the East. We were told it was the Island of Malta. As we got closer, we could see a whole bunch of ships sailing out towards us. Then we were told they were English and Canadian troop ships. And Malta was the rendezvous point. This was late afternoon July 9, 1943. From there we sailed to Sicily, which is about 90 miles away, and made the D-Day invasion of Sicily. On the way to Sicily the water became very rough. I was on a larger Navy ship, so it wasn't too bad. But sailing along side of us, on both sides, were small Infantry landing craft, loaded with First Division Infantry soldiers. We were all very close, and I could see the small landing craft, bouncing up and down on the waves. And most of the soldiers were sea sick, leaning over the side and throwing up.

Then early the next morning, we all made the D-Day invasion of Sicily, which was July 10, 1943. The First Division assault waves landed at 2:45 AM. The First Division on the South shore of Sicily, just to the East of the town of Gela.

Lieutenant Colonel William O'Darby and his U.S. Rangers, better known as "Darby's Rangers" landed to our left at the town of Gela. And to our right, the U.S. Forty Fifth Infantry Division. Also, before we landed, about midnight, American paratroopers of the Eighty Second Airborne Division jumped inland a little north of the beach landings. All beach landings were successful. On our beach, the first wave of the 16th Infantry of the First Division encountered manned pill boxes, and machine gun nests, which they knocked out.

The English 8th Army landed simultaneously on the East side of Sicily with the Canadian Army.

When it was time for us to land, small landing craft pulled up along side of the large Navy ship I was on. And we all climbed down the huge cargo nets, attached to the side of the ship. While climbing down the cargo nets, we could hear small arms fire on the beach. When we boarded the small landing craft, I don't remember what time it was. I think it was about 5:30

AM. We got ashore okay. As soon as the sailors dropped the ramp, we all jumped off and ran ashore. There was very little shooting at that time. So we all ran as fast as we could to some sand dunes about five hundred feet from the water's edge. I didn't dig a fox hole, because I figured we wouldn't stay there long. I was correct. In about fifteen minutes the Sergeant told us we were moving out. We went single file about twenty yards apart. I felt like a big shot, he didn't tell me to carry the stretcher with the big medical trunk on it. We kept moving inland. After awhile some German planes came over and bombed and strafed the beach. Then a little later, the enemy artillery opened up and started shelling the beach. After a while, the big Navy guns started shelling. I guess they found out where the enemy artillery was located. About that time, the small arms fire increased. Both ours and the enemy. We could hear a lot of shooting straight ahead and to our left and right flanks. Now artillery fire was intensifying. We could hear tanks rumbling straight ahead. At this time, the First Division Infantry was engaging the German Infantry, supported by German tanks.

About noon, July 10, 1943, Darby's Rangers reported the town of Gela taken.

By night fall, the 16th Infantry of the First Division captured the town of Pina Lupo, which had been defended by about nineteen light tanks and infantry.

All during D-Day enemy tanks were beaten off or destroyed by Antitank Company and Cannon Company swapping shots, direct fire, with the German tanks. Also by infantry soldiers with bazookas firing direct fire at the tanks, and by mortars. Fighting continued the entire first night, with the infantry slowly advancing.

That first day, when the Medics left the beach single file, about twenty yards apart, we would stop every now and then to tend to the wounded. Finally we went into a big olive grove, and we were told to dig in which I did. That was my first fox hole in Sicily. It was kind of skimpy. I didn't dig too deep, because I thought we wouldn't stay there too long. I was wrong, we spent the whole first night there. But I never did go into my fox hole. Because all night long, there were jeeps and half-tracks running in and out and all around the olive grove. I was afraid they wouldn't see my fox hole and unintentionally run over, or into my fox hole; so I spent most of the night cat napping, sitting on the ground leaning up against an olive tree. In the morning we moved out single file again. We went about three quarters of a mile and again we were told to dig in; which we did. I just finished digging my fox hole when the Sergeant told a bunch of us to get stretchers and follow him. We went about three quarters of a mile, and saw a very sad sight. There was an American tank that had just been knocked out. It was all black, scorched, and smoking. There were about three American soldiers with their clothes all burnt off. Their clothes were lying on the ground smoking. They were completely naked except for their shoes, which they still had on. Their bodies were 100% burned. They were just sort of standing or bending over. They couldn't sit down, if their bodies touched against anything they would scream from the pain. There were a couple of riflemen up on top of the tank trying to get another burnt soldier out of the tank. He was also screaming from the pain. Finally they got him out. Now it was our turn to try to help them. It seemed like an impossible situation. So we gave them each a couple of shots of morphine to try and kill the pain, which didn't really work. Then two ambulances showed up with big jars of Sufadiazine ointment and a big box of tongue depressors, so we each took a jar of Sulfadiazine Ointment and tried to rub it on them using the tongue depressors, but each time we touched them with the tongue depressors, they would scream. So we threw the tongue depressors away and we just took handfuls of the Sulfadiazine Ointment and rubbed it all over their bodies as best we could. Every time we touched them, they would scream. We tried to get them on the stretchers, but it was too painful. Only one of them was able to get on a stretcher, but he couldn't lie down. He sort of knelt down on it, so we put him in the ambulance. The others were unable to get on the stretchers due to severe pain. We helped them as best we could. Finally they were all in the ambulances and they left.

George A. Flynn

At that point, I said a prayer for them. I also said, "Please God, if you want me, take me, but please don't let that happen to me." I really don't know what happened to them, but months later I heard a rumor that one of them lived. After the ambulances left, we went back to the First Aid station. There I was assigned as a litter bearer, also administering first aid as required. As the rifle companies advanced, from one hill to another, so did the First Aid station, always one or two hills behind the Infantry. The Rifle Companies kept us busy. They were our best customers. Every time we had to move the First Aid station, it consisted of taking the First Aid tent apart, putting it on a jeep, or carrying it on a stretcher, depending on the terrain, or the present situation.

A very unfortunate and tragic thing happened regarding American Paratroopers in Sicily. It went like this. As I mentioned before, the 82nd Airborne Parachute Division, made their first jump in Sicily a few hours before the First Infantry Division and other American, Canadian, and English Infantry units made their landings about 2:45 A.M. on July 10, 1943. That jump was okay, it went according to schedule.

The problem was all American forces in Sicily were told on our second day in Sicily, that on the second night in Sicily more American Paratroopers would be dropped about midnight. We were all told not to shoot at airplanes or paratroopers, but none were dropped that second night. So we

30

all figured the drop was canceled indefinitely and completely. But the problem happened on the third night.

After three days in Sicily, I was very tired and sleepy. That night I must have lain down and went right off to sleep, because I didn't hear anything that night. But when I woke up about 5:00 A.M., everybody told me what happened during the night. They told me that about midnight a lot of airplanes started flying over and everybody started shooting at them, as they flew in from Africa over the Mediterranean Sea, the American Navy and American Merchant Marine ships were shooting at them, American antiaircraft crews on the beach were shooting at them, then as they got inland all the American Infantry outfits on the front lines also were shooting at them. As a result a lot of the airplanes were shot down with the paratroopers still in the airplanes. A lot of the paratroopers were killed and some severely wounded while still in the airplanes before they got to their drop zones. As a result, a lot of the paratroopers started jumping out of the airplanes early, before they got to their scheduled drop zones, as they floated down they were being shot at by both American Infantry soldiers, who thought they were German paratroopers, and the whole German Army was also shooting at them, because the Germans knew that no German paratroopers were scheduled to jump that night.

It turned out that all American outfits, Army, Navy, and Merchant Marine were all told that American paratroopers were scheduled to jump on the third night in Sicily.

So exactly what caused the disaster, is probably disputed to this very day.

Was it a lack of complete communication? Very possible. Or was it caused by a nervous antiaircraft gunner? Also very possible.

I remember one time in Sicily, we had to move the First Aid station about five miles up and down big hills and I mean big hills, sort of like small mountains. I got stuck carrying the same big medical trunk loaded with what, I never did find out. But I suspect it could have been a big metal dental chair that I saw being used a few times, or could it have been the Officer's liquor rations? I, and another soldier had to carry it up and down all those big hills. It was a very hot day, to say the least, I was very uncomfortable. But as heavy as it was, every now and then we would pass a small house, and they all had gardens and as we would pass the gardens, we would pick some tomatoes and melons and put them on the stretcher, with the big heavy trunk. When we would pass the next garden, we would pick more tomatoes and melons. Every time the column would stop for a rest, or what have you, we would eat some tomatoes and melons. When we passed the next garden we would pick some more tomatoes and melons. When we arrived at our planned location we would have to dig fox holes and set up the First Aid tent. I was thinking I would have to walk all the way through Sicily carrying that stretcher and big medical trunk. The way I had to that night in Africa.

About the fourth night in Sicily, I was sound asleep in my fox hole, when there was all kinds of explosions, the sky was all lit up. It looked like a Grucci fireworks display, and was about two miles away. We were told the German artillery had hit our gasoline and ammunition dumps.

But then one day, they sent me as a First Aid man to Cannon Company. I loved that promotion because Cannon Company didn't have to walk up and down the hills. They rode on half-tracks and full-tracks. I think the half-tracks had a seventy five millimeter gun and a few fifty caliber machine guns on them. If I remember correctly.

The full-tracks had a 105 millimeter cannon, and a few fifty caliber machine guns on board. I felt like a big shot riding instead of walking. But as they say, All's fair in love and war.

The war became a lot more interesting with Cannon Company, than as a litter bearer with the First Aid station. Maybe because I wasn't so tired and worn out running up and down the hills carrying the wounded on a stretcher.

With Cannon Company you pull into a field, fire the cannon for awhile, pack up and go to another hill or field, fire the cannon, maybe stay for a day or so, then go to another location and do the same thing. But at each location, after the half-tracks and full-tracks were set up, the next thing was to dig your fox hole. It turned out I dug more fox holes with Cannon Company, than with the First Aid station. But I wasn't as tired with Cannon Company because when we changed locations, I rode in the full-track, whereas, with the First Aid station, every time we moved, I had to carry the stretcher with the big medical trunk on it. I thanked the Lord for that move. Of course, being with Cannon Company wasn't the safest place in the world. If we moved from one location to another on dusty roads, or dried out fields, the half-tracks and full-tracks would leave a cloud of dust. And the enemy would see the dust, and know where we were. Then in would come the mortars and artillery shells. But then our Officers on the O.P. (Observation Post) would find out where the enemy was. And now it would be our turn to shell them. And if we moved the half-tracks and full-tracks at night, or on a rainy day, we wouldn't leave the dust trails for the enemy to see. But the half-tracks and full-tracks made so much noise when moving from one location to another, the enemy could hear us, and the shelling would start again.

But there was also many funny things that happened during the war. I remember a very funny thing that happened. One night, we pulled into a small Sicilian town. I don't remember if I was a litter bearer, or with

Cannon Company at the time. But anyhow, at the far end of town, there was a big cement thing, like a small pool. It was about twenty feet wide and about forty feet long. It was about two and a half feet deep. At one end was a pipe up higher than the pool. It was feeding water into the pool. We were all hot, sweaty, and dirty. So at first light, we all took our clothes off and were all ready to jump into the pool but somebody hollered wait, don't jump in. We asked why. He said there are funny looking things in the pool. Somebody else said they looked like leaches. So we didn't jump into the pool. Instead, we all stood around using our helmets to draw water and rinse off. When we were done, the entire pool was full of soapy water. We all felt very refreshed after our early morning bath. About an hour later, the townspeople started coming there with big jars. They looked at the water, and started pointing at the water, and hollering at us. We all started laughing because they were hollering in Italian and we couldn't understand. The whole thing seemed so funny. Then a shepherd showed up with a small flock of sheep. The sheep ran up to the pool, they looked and smelled at the water, but they wouldn't drink it. Now the sheep and the townspeople are all mad at us. They are all running around making noise. Finally one of the townspeople who could speak English showed up. He took one look at the pool then he started to laugh. He spoke to the townspeople in Italian then they all quieted down. Then he spoke to us in English. He explained, this is where they had to come to get their drinking water. They would come here and fill up their jugs every morning, and the sheep were also brought here for water. Now we understood what all the commotion was about. As we were leaving, the people were trying to splash the soapy water out of the pool. We went a little further, and we saw another shepherd, with another small flock of sheep heading towards the pool. As we were leaving, one of our guys said, "No wonder the Germans evacuated this town, you can't even take a bath here."

I remember one night outside the Sicilian town of Troina we set up in the night time. And when it got bright in the morning, we found ourselves set up right near the top of this big hill or mountain or whatever you would call it. We looked around, and we could see the tops of all the other big hills or mountains, or whatever they were. We were just getting out of our fox holes when all hell broke loose. Artillery shells were coming in all over our location. We knew we were under direct observation. Shells were hitting all over the place. Some of our guys just lay on the ground and couldn't get back to their fox holes. Those that were near their fox holes jumped in and stayed there. It turned out that there was a ten foot deep gully about sixty feet long near the top of the ridge where we were. So most of us ended up in that gully. They shelled us for about two hours. Then they slowed down their shelling. At that time, our drivers ran and moved the half-tracks and full-tracks back down the hill, out of direct observation. About that time, somebody from another hill spotted where the German artillery was dug in. Then we shelled them for about an hour. The amazing thing about this three hour artillery duel, was that not one of our guys got hit. And none of our vehicles were knocked out. They were hit by flying shrapnel, but still operable. I guess the Good Lord was on our side that day. Boy what a nice feeling it was to get off the top of that hill or mountain, or whatever it was.

A few days later, I went back to the First Aid station to get more medical supplies. While there, the litterbearers brought a small Italian boy, about seven or eight years old, in on a stretcher. He had half of his leg blown off. They said he stepped on a land mine. His mother and father were walking next to the stretcher. It was a sad sight. I got my medical supplies, and went back to Cannon Company.

For the next week or so everything was pretty routine. Pull into a field, set up, shoot the cannons, it was sort of a routine performance.

We finally ended up at the Southwest corner of Mt. Etna. We were there for about a day or so, when we were told the Germans had pulled out of Sicily. They evacuated into Italy. So that meant the Sicilian campaign was over.

That's when we started drinking a lot of wine, vino, as they called it. We stayed at the base of Mt. Etna for a week or so. Being that the shooting was over, we walked partly up Mt. Etna. We were walking on old lava flows. You could see how the lava had just flowed down the mountain. It was very interesting. In between the lava flows, wherever there was soil, there were blackberries growing. Everyday I went up the hill and picked a helmet full of blackberries. One day the cooks served us blue mashed potatoes. We asked how come the mashed potatoes were blue. They said one of the cooks got drunk, and dumped a five gallon can of vino in with the mashed potatoes. They tasted delicious. Everybody went back for seconds.

A few days later, we were sent back to Southern Sicily, near where we had made the D-Day invasion. When we arrived there, I had to leave Cannon Company, because all the medics were put together as a group in this big olive grove. We set up this big First Aid tent. Then we all spread out and set up pup tents under the olive trees so if German planes came over, they couldn't see us. We stayed there about a month, while they decided what to do with us. By that, I don't just mean the medics; the entire First Infantry Division.

The entire Division was all around there someplace all living in pup tents under olive trees. Good thing the Italians like olives, otherwise we wouldn't have had enough trees to hide under.

While there I met my old friend Sergeant Stanley Pearby, who I first met in Africa when I first joined the Big Red One. Sergeant Stanley Pearby was also a medic with the 16<u>th</u> Infantry of the First Division. He was not a rookie like me. He was an old timer, and was a regular Army career soldier. He was a medic with the First Division before the war started. He went overseas with the First Division and fought in all eight campaigns, starting with the D-Day invasion of Africa, at Arzue just outside of Oran. Pearby liked a drink of booze whenever available. I suppose that is why he and I became good friends. After a few weeks in the olive groves, one day a few of us were sitting around sipping vino. I asked if the story I heard about Pearby was true. The story about booze bottles and the hypodermic needles. They all laughed and assured me that story was true. Sergeant Guretsky told the story. He said it went like this. The Officers got a liquor ration and the enlisted men didn't get a liquor ration. Therefore, after a few weeks in Africa, a few of the medical officers started to complain. A few of them asked Sergeant Pearby, how come the seals on their booze bottles weren't broken but it looked like a few ounces were missing out of each bottle. Sergeant Pearby said "I don't know, after all this is Africa, maybe the heat evaporated the booze." That went on all through the African campaign. Then one night somebody spotted Sergeant Pearby sticking a large thick hypodermic needle through the seal, through the cork and extracting the booze. It seems everybody knew about it, but nobody ever squealed. I said "Pearby did you do that?" He said "George, how could you even think I would do such a thing." I don't think it happened in Sicily, because it was easy to get wine in Sicily. At this point, I would like to mention that Sergeant Geretzky if I remember correctly, his first name was Mike. He was also an old timer with the First Division. He went through all eight campaigns. I don't know if he was drafted or volunteered to join the Army, but I do know he was a school teacher in Rochester, New York before the war. He told me he was keeping a daily diary about all the battles and everything that happened from day to day including people's names and locations of towns. I don't know if he ever did write a book, but he told me he was going to write a book based on his diary when the war ended. If he did write a book, I would love to read it. His book could be adopted as an actual history of the First Division in World War Two. He was a non-nonsense sort of guy. If he wrote a book, it would be nothing but actual facts and dates according to his diary. Whereas me writing this book, I never kept a diary. I am writing more than fifty years after the War ended, relying on memory only.

Then one day, while still camped in the olive grove, they told us the Army was sending a bunch of Army doctors to Sicily to give every First Division soldier a physical examination to see if we were physically fit for more combat. First they checked the Officers. Then they started checking the non-commissioned officers. They never did get down to the lower ranks. A few days later the visiting Army doctors left. A few days later we heard that the visiting doctors decided that we were physically unfit for more combat. We heard that there was a very high percentage of Malaria among those tested.

We had expected to be sent into Italy to continue fighting the German Army. So at this point, the Army didn't know what to do with the First Infantry Division. Therefore, we stayed in Sicily under the almond trees, for another month. We drank a lot of wine, ate a lot of almonds and played a lot of cards.

One day while we were there, we got paid, I think it was two months pay, and that night we drank a lot of wine. There were a few craps and card games going one, due to being paid that day. I never shot craps and very seldom played cards. But that night I guess due to drinking a lot of wine, I decided to play cards. There was a big Blackjack game going on. I knew how to play blackjack, but I had never played for dollars. In the past, I had only played for nickels and dimes, but this night the dollars must have caught my eye so I joined in. We played for a couple of hours. I must have had too much wine during the card game because the next morning I had an awful hang over and I didn't remember leaving the card game, or going back to my pup tent. When I woke up the next morning in my pup tent, I had to blow my nose, so I reached into my pocket to get a handkerchief, and what came out of my pockets was paper. I couldn't find my handkerchief. Finally I sat up and looked at all paper lying on the ground in my pup tent. To my surprise it was all brand new Italian paper money, which we had been paid the day before. I said to myself "Gee, I must have won the card game," but I couldn't remember. So I left my pup tent and went to wash up. On the way, I met some of the other soldiers who had been in the card game the night before. When I said good morning to them, they said they never saw anything like it. They said I just kept winning almost every hand. They said I would have two tens, and ask for another card and I would get an ace. They said, no matter what I did, I couldn't lose. I think I won over four hundred dollars. I don't think I ever played cards again. I sent all the money home to my mother. I knew she needed it more than I did.

Early one morning I was still asleep in my pup tent when all of sudden I woke up and heard what I thought were small stones hitting my pup tent. I looked out and started laughing. The olive grove was full of civilians; men, women, and children. The men had long bamboo poles and they were hitting them up high on the olive trees. It was harvest time and the olives were falling all over the place.

CHAPTER FOUR:

ENGLAND

One day we were loaded onto ships again. We thought maybe we would be shipped back to the States. No such luck. We were sent to England. This was my first visit to England. But for the old soldiers of the First Division it was their second visit to England. When they first went overseas from the States they sailed to England on board the former luxury liner, the Queen Mary which was converted to a troop ship at the beginning of World War Two. When they were sent to England the first time it was to prepare for the D-Day invasion of North Africa - Now here is the First Division, back in England. This time to prepare for the Normandy Invasion. The ship I arrived on in England,docked in Liverpool. There we boarded trains and were sent to Southern England for two reasons; number one being, at that time it was still possible that Germany would still invade England, and if so the First Division would be there to greet them. Reason number two was because it was a good place to practice amphibious maneuvers to prepare for the D-Day Invasion of France. I ended up in the small town of Beamster. The English people were very friendly. When they got to know us, most of them asked what kind of people we were. They said they never saw people with blue gums, tongues, and lips before. We laughed and told them it was because of all the wine we drank in Sicily after the campaign ended. It took a month or so before our gums, lips and tongues return to their natural color. Those that drank the most, took the longest to return their natural color.

The town of Beamster was a typical, quaint, small, English town. It had about four pubs. If I remember correctly, I think the pub names were The Red Lion Inn, The Nags Head Inn, The Crown Head Inn. And - ? Can't remember the last one. Because of the War, everything in England was rationed including beer. As a result, the pubs in Beamster would run out of beer about two days before the next week's ration. As a result, a lot of the soldiers would go to the next closest town, which was the town of Crewkerne, it was about seven miles away. It was off limits to the First Division and as a result, we all became very good sewers. If the MP's saw a First Division soldier in Crewkerne they would tell us to leave. So whenever we went to Crewkerne, Step #1 we had to cut our Big Red number one shoulder patch off our left shoulder. Next Step #2. No matter what, the shoulder patch had to be sewed back on, for inspection the next morning. So that made us champion sewers. Even though Crewkerne was off limits, we were usually given transportation both ways. But the truck going back left at a certain time and if you missed it, you had a seven mile walk, which we made many a night.

While in England, Cannon Company was given new cannons, 105 mm. Short barrel Howitzers and half-tracks to pull them. Cannon Company was sent to an English artillery range in Wales, and being a Cannon Company medic, I went with them. We stayed about a week in Wales shooting and getting familiar with the new cannons.

One day while still in Wales we were taken out in the woods, hiking up and down a bunch of big hills. We stayed out in the woods all day, until it got dark. Then we were led back to a paved road, where trucks were waiting to take us back to the English soldier's barracks where we were staying. There was about six inches of snow on the ground, and it was very cold. There we loaded onto the trucks real quick to keep warm. We drove about five miles back to the barracks. When we arrived back at the barracks as soon as we jumped off the trucks, we had to line up and they took a roll call. As a result of the roll call, it was determined that one soldier was missing. The missing soldier was Mokowitz. I don't remember if he was a Private, Corporal or a Sergeant at that time. I do remember that he was the radio operator with Cannon Company which was a very dangerous job. It consisted of going on the O.P. (Observation Post) with the Cannon Company Officer who was directing the cannon firing onto the German

Infantry, or whatever other targets he could see such as German mortar crews, German artillery positions, or German tanks.

Now we are still lined up and standing at attention near the trucks we just jumped off. I think, at that time, we were all thinking the same thing. How nice it would be to get into the nice warm mess hall and have some hot chow. But it didn't go that way. Now it was time for Captain O'Brien to take over, which we all knew he would do. We all knew we would get a ream job. But we all figured he would also make it comical, which he did. Captain O'Brien started walking up and down looking at us and shaking his head. Finally he said, "I know what happened when you all came out of the woods, and it was time to board the trucks you were cold and hungry. Some of you probably knew that Mokowitz was missing and what do you do? Did you report him missing? No, nobody reported him missing and I know what you did, you all said - F- Mokowitz-Chow. And you all came back here for chow. That's not the way it works. Everybody back on the trucks and don't come back until you find Mokowitz." So we all jumped on the trucks. They took us back to where they had picked us up. We all split up into small groups, and back into the woods we all went, searching and calling Mokowitz. We kept walking up and down hills searching and calling for Mokowitz. After about three hours, we were ordered out of the woods, and back to the road. This time they took a roll call. Everybody was present except Mokowitz. While we were standing at attention, after the roll call, we were told that Mokowitz was safe and sound, back in the barracks. We were told that when Mokowitz came out of the woods, we had all left in the trucks. Mokowitz started to walk back to the barracks. After a while a British Army truck came by and gave him a lift back to the barracks. When he arrived back at the barracks, there was nobody there, we were all out in the woods looking for him. So he took a shower and then went to the mess hall and had a nice hot meal. We all had a good laugh, everybody including Mokowitz. Naturally from then on, whenever it was chow time, everybody would holler. "F-Mokowitz - Chow," including Mokowitz. Mokowitz was a very good and brave soldier. On D-Day in Normandy, France he was awarded a very high medal for bravery. I don't remember exactly what medal he received. But I know it was a very high medal.

All told, we must have stayed about six months in England. Then one day we were told to pack up, we are moving out, and not coming back to Beamster. So we went to what they called the staging areas in Southern England closer to the English Channel. The staging areas were in preparation for loading on ships, for the impending invasion of Europe. We stayed in the staging area for about three weeks. Then we were sent to the port, at either Portland or Weymouth. We were given what was called two and a half ton Ducks. They were like a boat, with big tires and wheels.

They could be used in the water as a boat, and on land as a truck. They are designed to just drive out of the water and onto the land without stopping.

CHAPTER FIVE:

D-DAY

Normandy France

When leaving England, we drove the Ducks down to the dock, and then drove them onto a big Navy landing craft. While sitting on the duck at the dock, waiting to load onto the big Navy landing craft, one of our Privates said, "Hey Sergeant I lost my leggings, do I have to go?" The Sergeant said, "I'll loan you my leggings." We all got a good laugh at that. We all remembered what happened in Africa, when Captain O'Brien was inspecting his Cannon Company soldiers on the dock in Algiers. One soldier didn't have his leggings on, and Captain O'Brien wouldn't let him make the D-Day invasion in Sicily, because he was improperly dressed. He had to come ashore the second day with the kitchen crew.

Each Duck had a 105 mm cannon. The cannon was not part of the Duck. The cannon was picked up by a crane and then lifted onto the Duck. Then about a hundred rounds, maybe more of 105 mm artillery shells were also loaded onto the Duck. Each round weighed about thirty pounds. I

49

don't know how much the cannon weighed. I guess it must have weighed a couple of thousand pounds. So between the cannon and about a hundred or more rounds of ammunition for the cannon, that's a hell of a lot of weight.

We had about five or six Ducks with a cannon on each Duck. Then there was another Duck without a cannon on it, instead it had a small crane on it. If all went according to plan, which it didn't, the plan was supposed to work like this. When we got to shore, if necessary, we could fire the cannon as soon as we got out of the water and onto the beach. The cannon could be fired while still on the Duck if necessary. But what was hoped was, if possible, the Duck with the crane on it would pull along side of each Duck and unload the cannon. When it was time to move the cannon to a different location, attach the cannon to a hitch at the rear of the Duck and the Duck would pull the cannon to the next location. That's the way it was planned but it didn't work that way.

Well, when Cannon Company was all loaded onto the Navy landing ship, in England, we pulled out into the English Channel. I think we were on the Navy ship for two days. All that time the big convoy kept moving all different directions, I guess, so the Germans didn't know where we were going to land. The water in the Channel got very rough. All of a sudden we heard rifle shots. We all went up on deck, to see what was going on. Then we saw a sailor on an American Destroyer, shoot every now and then at something with a rifle. At first we didn't know what he was shooting at. Then we saw what he was shooting at as it bobbed up and down with the waves. It was a big black floating mine. He could only get a shot in every now and then he had to wait until it went down on the low side of the wave, if he shot at it when it was on top of the wave, he could have hit somebody on another ship. There were ships all over the place. Next, all of the ships started to steer clear of the mine. Next a small mine sweeper started to move in on the mine. We didn't hear an explosion, so I guess they picked it up.

Now it is D-DAY NORMANDY France June 6, 1944.

The First Infantry Division, of which I am a part, was scheduled to land on Omaha Beach. The first wave was scheduled to land at 6:30 AM. Cannon Company 16th Infantry Regiment of the First Infantry Division of which I am a part was scheduled in the third wave, about an hour after the first wave. The English and the Canadian Armies were scheduled to land East of the First Division. The American 29th Infantry Division was scheduled to land West of the First Division. The American 4th Infantry Division was scheduled to land West of the 29th Division. The American Rangers were scheduled to land three miles west of the 4th Division.

Now this is what happened to me on D-Day June 6, 1944. I am one of the First Aid men with Cannon Company 16th Infantry Regiment of the First

Infantry Division. We are on a large Navy landing ship. About 2:00 AM, June 6, 1944, we are told to get on board our two and a half ton Duck, which goes in the water as a boat, and on land as a truck. There must have been about twelve soldiers on each duck, plus the cannon and ammunition for the cannon. We are sitting in the Duck, when all of a sudden, there is a commotion. Somebody started loading cartons of food on each Duck. The cartons were standard size about 1 1/2 feet x 1 1/2 feet about 3 feet long. We ended up with about four cartons on our Duck. I don't know if the soldiers broke into the Navy storeroom, of if the sailors felt sorry for us, and just gave us the cartons of food. All of a sudden, the Navy ship stopped, and cut off their motors and it became very quiet. When that happened, all of a sudden they dimmed all the lights in the hold of the ship where we were, and it became very dark and it was hard to see. Then all of a sudden the big landing ramp opened and was lowered into the water. I looked out when the ramp was lowered, it was pitch dark outside, and I couldn't see anything. And inside the Navy ships there was only a very dim light. At that moment, it was sort of an eerie feeling. Then orders were given for the Ducks to drive off the ramp and into the pitch dark water. The plan was for the Ducks to go out a few hundred feet and keep circling around, until all the Ducks were in the water, then head for the beach.

The big Navy ship let us off ten miles out. The idea was to surprise the enemy. Less chance of the Ducks being seen than the big Navy ships. That part worked fine.

Now the first Duck got off the big Navy ship without a problem. Next was the second Duck, the one I was on. The motor started up right away, and we drove off the ramp and into the water, no problem. We could see the first Duck about a hundred feet in front of us. But then it happened. Our rudder must have jammed, because our Duck would only pull to the right, it wouldn't go straight ahead, and it wouldn't go to the left. So we just went around in a semi-circle, and we bumped into the middle of the big Navy ship that we had just gotten off of. When all the Ducks were in the water the sailors threw us a rope and pulled us around to the landing ramp. They tried to fix the rudder, but couldn't. Then all the other Cannon Company Ducks, that were in the water, were told to head for the beach. We asked the Navy Officer, "What about us?" He said to wait where we were. He said they have a lot of extra small landing craft circling around to pick up survivors, in case some ships got torpedoed or hit by artillery, or whatever. He said we came under the whatever category. He signaled one of them, and told them what happened to us and told them what to do. It was a small Infantry Landing craft. There were three or four sailors on it. So they tried to fix our rudder, but couldn't. So the Officer told them to pull us to shore. So they tied a big long thick rope from the back of their landing craft, to the front of our Duck and they started pulling us.

Everything is okay now, it is still dark and no shooting yet. The Germans don't know we are here yet. The water is getting kind of choppy now. Everything is going good, nice and peaceful. One of our guys in a very low voice, started to sing. "While Paddling Madeline Home," nobody joined in, we just listened. Then after awhile the Duck started to make water, up through the floor boards. Also, due to the weight of the cannon, and having about a hundred or more rounds of ammunition for the cannon, mind you each round weighed about thirty pounds and the water was getting choppy, and every now and then a small wave hits us broadside and comes in over the top. The water is also still coming up through the floor boards. Staff Sergeant Motolowski, who is in charge tells us to take our helmets off and start bailing the water out, which we did. We held our own for awhile, but not too long. It is still dark and no shooting yet.

Sergeant Motolowski was a very brave and good soldier and was well liked. He was also a good friend of mine. After awhile, I said to Sergeant Mot. "I don't know if you know anything about boats." He said "Not too much." I said, "I know a little about boats, but not too much either. But one thing I can tell you, this Duck is greatly overloaded and as a result we are sitting too low in the water Mot, we will never make it to shore this thing is going to sink." He said, "What can we do?" I said, "We must throw the ammunition overboard. The lighter we make it, the higher the Duck will ride in the water. That will stop the water from coming over the top every time a wave hits us broadside. Then with bailing out we should be okay." He gave orders to throw the cartons of food overboard. I said "The food is light, the ammo is heavy." He said, "George you know the orders. You can throw your shoes, helmet, and clothes away, but don't dare throw your gun or ammo away. You want to come in bare ass - okay. But make sure you have your gun and ammo." I said, "I know, but I think it better to get in with the cannon and one round. Than leave everything out here." So we all kept bailing.

After awhile it became very obvious that the Duck was going to sink, and very soon. At that point Mot said, "Start throwing the ammo overboard." I said "It's too late, this thing is going down." So I stood up and said, "I know some of you can't swim, but you all have life savers on and all you have to do is jump in head first, as if you are sliding into home plate, and swim as far away from here as possible because when the Duck goes under there will be a big undertow. And if you are too close it will pull you under also. You have life preservers on, so your head will stay above water. Then paddle back to the Navy landing craft, that was pulling us. The sailors will pick us up." At that point, I was the first to jump into the water.

When I thought I was far enough away, I turned around to see what was happening. I said, "Oh my God," when I saw what was happening. What I saw was the rear of the Duck, was slowly going under the water and the front of the Duck was way up high in the air and the tow line was still tied to the front of the Duck which was way up high in the air. And the other end of the tow rope was still tied to the rear of the small Navy landing craft. As a result, the rear of the lighter Navy landing craft was being pulled out of the water, because it was still tied to the front of the Duck which was way up high in the air. But thanks to a quick acting sailor who had a big boughy knife and was chopping away at the tow rope. When he finally cut the tow rope, the rear of the Navy landing craft which was way up high in the air, came crashing down into the water with a tremendous splash and bang. At about the same time the front of the Duck went up a little higher in the air. And then the back of the Duck started to slowly sink into the water. In about two minutes the Duck, cannon and about a hundred rounds of ammo were all gone.

Now I was about twenty yards away from the small Navy landing craft which had been pulling the Duck. The clamps which were holding my May West life preserver together had broken before I jumped in the water, and it kept slipping off as I tried to swim. I had to swim with one hand, and try to hold the life preserver on with the other hand. I never was a good swimmer, so by the time I reached the small Navy landing craft, I was kind of tired. The sailors didn't open the landing ramp, so we had to climb up and over the side of the landing craft. That wasn't easy because it was at least four feet above the water. When I got there, one of our soldiers was on the landing craft and he was pulling and helping the second soldier up and onto the landing craft. When I got there, he pulled and helped me onto the landing craft. I don't think I could have climbed up and aboard without his help. When I got on board, I helped him pull two more soldiers out of the water, and up onto the landing craft. By that time, my arms became very tired, I didn't have the strength to help him pull anybody else on board, I just fell onto the floor, gasping for air. The soldier that pulled me out of the water didn't stop until everybody was out of the water and safely aboard the landing craft. His name is Sergeant Langford he is very strong, and was a former prize fighter. I know if it wasn't for Sergeant Langford, a few of us would have drowned including myself. He should have been awarded a medal for saving lives that day. As far as I know, he was never awarded anything for saving Cannon Company lives that day.

When we were all aboard the landing craft Sergeant Mot, took a roll call. One soldier was missing, so he told the sailors to circle around to see if we could find him.

Another soldier, Corporal Pluggy Kluze, told us he himself was the last man to jump overboard and Kluze said that just before he jumped overboard, there was still one soldier left on the Duck. It was Private Leonard. Kluze told Leonard, "It's starting to sink, we must jump." But Private Leonard said, "I can't, my legging is caught on the camouflage net, and I can't get it loose." Kluze tried to help him, but the duck started to sink. And Kluze had to jump overboard. That was the last time Little Private Leonard was ever seen. The landing craft circled around but we couldn't find Leonard.

I still wonder to this day if it was possible for the sailors to have lowered the ramp door, so we didn't have to climb up four feet, over the side of the landing craft. If the ramp door was lowered we could have just crawled aboard. Maybe, because we were still about eight miles out from shore.

After unsuccessfully looking for Leonard, the landing craft started heading for shore. We are all soaking wet. No guns, no ammo, no medical supplies. My helmet fell off as I jumped off the Duck.

The sailors, after awhile, told us they couldn't take us any further. They said their job was to keep circling around, out where they picked us up. And they couldn't take us any further. They said they had to keep circling around looking for disabled landing craft and also looking for anybody that might be overboard.

Sergeant Mot said, "How are we going to get to shore?" They said they would signal another small landing craft, which was heading to the beach, which they did. So we pulled along side of another small landing craft that was full of soldiers heading towards the beach. So we all climbed aboard. When we were aboard the new landing craft we saw that they were not First Division soldiers. They were a Rifle Company of the 29th Infantry Division. Sergeant Mot told the sailors that we were First Division soldiers, and asked the sailors if they could put us on a First Division landing craft. The sailors said that where we were, there is only 29th Division landing craft. Then Sergeant Mot asked the sailors, if after they landed the 29th Division soldiers, could they take us to the First Division beach. The sailor said that when he lands the 29th Division soldiers, our beach would be only three miles to the left. He said we could walk to our beach. We all laughed and told him we would let him know after we see what the beach looks like. The 29th Division soldiers asked why we were all soaking wet. We told them what happened.

About that time all hell started to break loose. The big guns on the battleships started to open up. Then after a while the German artillery started to wake up. Now everybody is shooting at everybody. At this point,

I thought this is no place for Mrs. Flynn's little boy Georgie to be, but here I am. This was the first action for the 29th Infantry Division. And they knew we had fought in Africa and Sicily, so as we got closer to the beach they asked what the different shooting noises were. We told them, "That's our Navy shelling shore batteries. The other noise is the German artillery shelling our Navy ships." Another noise we told them were German mortars exploding on the beach. Then there was another noise, they asked about, and we told them that it was a German machine gun and that it shoots faster than our machine guns, and because it makes a different noise, we call it a burp gun.

Now we are getting real close to the beach. There was a Lieutenant in charge of the 29th Infantry Company who told his men to get ready to jump off as soon as the sailors let the ramp down. There was an awful lot of shooting at this point. German mortars and artillery were exploding all along the beach and in the water. Every now and then a machine gun bullet or rifle bullet would hit the landing craft. All of a sudden the sailors said, "This is it." And they lowered the ramp.

Now we could see what was happening. I think this was about an hour after the first wave hit the beach. And no American soldiers were on the beach yet. They were kneeling or standing in the water, shooting at the Germans. What I saw was about four hundred feet of sand, and past the sandy beach was nothing but cliffs almost straight up. The German infantry must have been dug in all over the cliffs. The German riflemen and machine gunners were having a hay day. It was like target practice for them. There were bodies floating all over the place. Some face up and some face down. When the ramp opened, nobody got off, everybody just looked. The only movement on the landing craft was a few of the soldiers that were in the water, trying to get on the landing craft. The Lieutenant pulled his tommy gun, and pointed it at those trying to get on the landing craft, and told them to get off, or he would shoot them. Then he looked at his men on the landing craft and told them to get off. No argument, they all got off. Then Sergeant Mot said to him, "What about us?" He told Sergeant Mot that was his decision. Sergeant Mot told him that if we are to be killed, he preferred to be killed on a First Division beach. The Lieutenant told us to only pick up the wounded which we did. Then the sailors closed the ramp and we left. As we were leaving it sounded like the Fourth of July. Artillery and mortars were exploding all over the place. Every now and then a bullet would hit the landing craft. I didn't have any first aid equipment, but we did what we could for the wounded, which wasn't much.

Sergeant Mot told the sailors that if they see a First Division landing craft, to let us get on it. They said okay, but their main objective was to go out to one of the big hospital ships for the wounded. And that's exactly what happened.

At this point, before I say what happened at the hospital ship, in regards to the bloody beach we just left. A few days later I was told that so many American soldiers were killed on that beach, that they stopped sending in more troops. Instead, when a beach head to the East was secured, they worked their way along the hill tops to the West. When the American soldiers looked down from the top of the cliff and saw nothing but dead American soldiers, I doubt if they took many prisoners that day.

When we got to the big hospital ship, we pulled alongside and they lowered the basket stretchers. We put the wounded on the basket stretchers, and they were lifted up onto the big hospital ship. When all the wounded were off our small landing craft, the sailors started to pull away, then somebody on the hospital ship told the sailors to stop. They did, and when we looked up there was a full medical Colonel leaning over the rail. He asked about the soldiers on the landing craft. Sergeant Mot told him that we weren't wounded. We still had to make the landing.

He asked why we were all wet. We told him what happened, that our Duck sank. He said his orders are to pick up all wounded and if any soldiers were on a craft that sank and were thrown into the water, he was also told to pick them up and take them back to England. We all looked at each other and started to laugh. We talked it over, and it was decided that if we went back to England Captain O'Brien would personally skin us alive. So Sergeant Mot told the Colonel, "Thanks, but we were okay, and we had to make the landing." Sergeant Mot then told the sailors to take us to shore at the First Division beach. They said if they saw another small landing craft, they would ask them to take us.

After a while, they signaled another small landing craft, and pulled along side of it. We were told to get on that craft, which we did. On the back of the small landing craft, on the floor, near where the sailors were was sort of a bench the width of the landing craft about a foot and a half high and about two feet deep. It had a small tarpaulin on it, sort of covering it. So about three or four of us sat on it. Now this small landing craft is taking us towards shore. After a while, I told the soldier next to me that I was getting hungry. He said he was also getting hungry. I said, "Let's look under this tarp, maybe we are sitting on C-rations." He said, "Good idea," so we lifted the tarp. I said, "Look at this, no end to the surprises today." Under the tarp, we found about six hundred, to a thousand bars of TNT - Each bar was about three inches long, two inches wide, and about three quarters of an inch thick. Each bar was separately wrapped and marked TNT. We showed it to Sergeant Mot. He asked the sailors what it was for. They said that they didn't know it was there. They said that the First

Division soldiers who they had taken to the beach earlier, must have left it there.

Sergeant Mot said that it was probably to blow up beach obstacles. He said when the soldiers saw what was going on, on the beach, they probably figured it was safer going ashore without the TNT so they left it on the landing craft. Sergeant Mot then said, "What I want you soldiers to do, is nice and slow, pick up one bar at a time and throw it overboard. Throw it a little way out from the landing craft. Remember, nice and slow. We all took turns throwing TNT overboard. After a while, the sailors told us they couldn't take us any further. I forgot what their reason was. So they signaled another landing craft, which was a much larger landing craft. I think it had a jeep and a truck on it. Our small landing craft pulled along side of the larger landing craft and we boarded it. And the larger landing craft took us all the way to the beach.

When the ramp opened, we all jumped off. The water was about waist deep. So we waded ashore and now I am on the First Division beach, which is called the Easy Red section of Omaha Beach. Then I ran as fast as possible and didn't do much looking around. I just ran straight ahead. I heard shells coming in, so I hit the dirt. After the shells exploded, I looked around and saw sort of a low spot about thirty yards ahead. So I ran for the low spot and hit the dirt again. I could hear shells going back and forth overhead. It was the German artillery shooting at the beach and also at the landing craft coming in. Also, our Navy shelling the Germans. I wouldn't be surprised if the Navy shells and the German shells, hit each other in mid air. They probably did.

So now I am lying on the ground, about sixty feet from the water's edge and I didn't have an entrenching tool to dig a fox hole with, so I started digging with my hands. There were a lot of beach stones that the tide must have washed in. After digging and throwing stones away for about fifteen minutes, I figured this is ridiculous. So I picked my head up and looked around a little more. About a hundred or a hundred and fifty feet to my left, and inland maybe a hundred more feet, I saw a circular mound. So I got up and ran as fast as I could towards the mound. Just before I got there more shells came in, so I hit the ground again. After they exploded I ran again towards the mound. As I got closer, I realized it was a pillbox, it looked like it had been knocked out by a flame thrower. The pillbox was elevated from the beach about fifteen or twenty feet and there was a cat walk around the beach side of the pillbox which was about four feet wide. I saw about five or six First Division Officers sitting on the cat walk, leaning against the pillbox. I said to myself, that cat walk looks like Heaven. So I ran as fast as I could for the pillbox and the cat walk. And I sat down about five feet from one of the Officers. He looked at me, and I looked at him. He didn't say anything and I didn't say anything.

Then a little later a few Cannon Company soldiers who landed with me spotted me and they came running across the beach, and joined me sitting on the cat walk. A little later a few more joined us.

So we just sat there watching a most unbelievable scene. After a while, I said to the Cannon Company soldier sitting next to me, if we had a movie camera, we could take movie pictures of what is going on. After the war, the pictures would be worth a fortune. He agreed with me. He then added, "If we just tell people what we are seeing they probably wouldn't believe us." So we just sat there and watched a most unbelievable scene. There was machine gun fire, mortar fire, artillery fire, and rifle fire. Our infantry was swapping shots with the German infantry who were dug in all over the hillsides, overlooking the beach.

Landing craft would come in to unload infantry soldiers and sometimes they would get blown up on the way in. Sometimes they would be able to unload the soldiers and then get hit on the way out. Then all of a sudden I realized there was some kind of medical unit coming along the beach with stretchers, they were coming from the East. They weren't First Division medics. They must have been some kind of an amphibious medical outfit. They were doing a terrific job, patching up the wounded, giving blood plasma, putting them on stretchers and carrying them along the beach to the East. There seemed to be some high sand dunes along that section of beach. They must have set up a First Aid station there. They were doing a wonderful job running back and forth taking care of the wounded.

After we were there for about an hour, the Rifle Companies must have taken some of the high ground overlooking the beach, because a little later, they started to bring some German soldiers who had surrendered, down on to the beach. When they got down on the beach, a couple of our soldiers who were guarding them didn't know what to do with them or where to take them. Everything was still being blown up. There was no place to go, so they just stood there looking at us and we were looking at them. I think at that point, they wished they hadn't surrendered. It was probably safer, up on the hill than down on the beach. They looked very nervous and scared. I guess they realized that they may be killed by their own artillery or mortars. After awhile our guys started moving the prisoners along the beach to the East towards where the medics were set up. Maybe somebody figured that if they had a bunch of German prisoners by the First Aid station, maybe the Germans would stop shelling that section of the beach. Every now and then, the Infantry would bring some more prisoners down to the beach.

After awhile, somebody called us. It was Staff Sergeant Biff Grimes. He had just came down to the beach from up the hill someplace. He asked if we were okay. We said, "Yes." Then he asked if we were able to get our cannon to shore. We told him, "No." The duck was overloaded and sank about eight miles out. I think he said they all sank. He then asked where the rest of our crew was. We told him that Private Leonard got his legging caught in the camouflage net and went down with the duck. We told him that the rest of us all landed together, but we don't know where they are now. He told us to wait here and he went looking for them. He found some of them and he knew the Officers who were on the cat walk with us, and he spoke to them for awhile. Then he told us to follow him single file about ten yards apart. He said we are going up the hill. At that point, there was a dirt road about twenty feet wide just to the left of the pillbox when you are looking up the hill.

Now, over fifty years later as I write this book, I realize for the first time, that I had or have some kind of a memory loss. What caused it I find a complete mystery. Never before did I ever realize or think about a memory loss. But now that I am trying to remember everything for the first time, I now realize that going up that dirt road from the beach to the top of the hill, I just can't remember anything. Possibly a huge shell exploded near me, and I blacked out from a concussion. But as my wife tells me, possibly as I started up the hill, I saw some very horrifying sights and my mind just blocked them out. I guess either explanation is a possibility. There is an old saying, "Let a sleeping dog sleep." Maybe I will enjoy the remainder of my life better not knowing what happened going up that hill that day. At this time, I just don't know if I should try to find out what happened, or if I should just forget about it.

The next thing I remember, it's dark, and I am digging a fox hole on top of the hill to the right of the dirt road, when facing South. I remember there was a very small farm house up near where I dug my fox hole.

As I sit here, now writing this book and trying to remember, I find it impossible to remember. Which means there is a period of about say eight to ten hours of missing time. Maybe a longer period, or maybe a shorter period.

When I finished digging my fox hole that first night, I must have slept like a baby. I probably lay down, stretched out and immediately fell asleep. If there was anymore shooting or noise that night, you can't prove it by me.

CHAPTER SIX:

FRANCE

Next morning I had to go down that same dirt road. I had to look for the First Aid station, to get medical supplies. About half way down the hill, coming up the hill, were about a dozen MP's with Tommy guns at the ready. They were spread out single file, on both sides of the road and in the middle of the road. All by himself, walking up the dirt road, was General Omar Bradley. He looked at me and said, "Soldier, where is your helmet?" I pointed out at the English Channel and said, "About eight miles out there Sir." He said, "Okay, but get one as soon as you can." I said, "Yes, Sir." No saluting in combat because the snipers like to shoot Officers, especially Generals. Then I proceeded down the hill to get medical supplies which I did. I also picked up a helmet lying on the beach and I had many to choose from. Now I am properly equipped. I have medical supplies and a helmet.

When I got back up the hill and rejoined Cannon Company, I was told now that we don't have any cannons, we are now a Rifle Company, until such time as we get cannons. So for about two weeks or so, we kept advancing along with the Rifle Companies.

Some things are hard to remember and sort of fuzzy in my mind. I remember bits and drabs of different things that happened, but not enough to put them in their correct sequence and chain of events. One such thing I remember from time to time, but can't really remember where or when it took place.

One time when I try to concentrate and remember where and when I think it happened on D-Day Normandy and another time I think it happened on maneuvers in England. I don't remember much about it. The thing that I do remember from time to time, is this. I am with Cannon Company. I don't remember if we had cannons or not. We are near the top of a big hill and we are looking at a bunch of ships out on the water and it seems to be early afternoon. Somebody came around and gave us each a can of unopened soup, it was an odd looking can. I had never seen one like it before. It had a wick sticking out of the top of the can. You lit the wick and it heated the soup. I think it was green pea soup. It was nice and hot and it was delicious. I loved it. We were told it was English soldiers rations. I remember sitting near the top or on the top of this very high hill, looking at all the ships out in the water. I know this happened but I don't know where.

Then one day we moved into a big field, and we were sitting around talking, when all of a sudden, we heard strange noises. It sounded like noise makers at a New Years Eve's party. Then we started to hear these strange noises all over the place. Then it dawned on us, what the strange noises were. They were noise makers that we carried in our gas masks only to be used if there was an actual gas attack by the enemy. The idea was, if there was a gas attack, the noise makers would alert everybody. So we did the same thing. We put on our gas masks and sat on the ground or a big rock, or whatever we could find to sit on. Then in our gas mask carrier, we each carried a clear cellophane cover, that we pulled down over our helmets, and pulled down over our enter bodies, so if gas was used, it couldn't get on our skin or clothes. It was the weirdest scene I had ever seen. All over this big field all you could see was soldiers with gas masks on, sitting on stones, or whatever, sitting under these transparent covers. We were all sitting there making as much noise as possible with our noise makers to alert the other soldiers in the area. It sounded like a million crickets all over the place. But there was a problem. After about five minutes under the protective clear covers, it got so hot that we all started to perspire and after a while it became impossible to breathe. So at this point, I had a choice suffocate under the protective cover, or take it off and maybe get burned by mustard gas. So at first, I lifted the transparent protective cover a few inches off the ground.

Nothing happened so I lifted it a little higher. The air felt so good and still nothing happened. So after awhile, I took it off completely. When I looked around, I saw the majority of the soldiers had also taken their protective covers off. Only a few were still sitting on the ground, under their protective covers, and sweating like mad. After awhile we heard the all clear signal. The next day we were told that a new outfit, just over from the States, were being shelled by the Germans, and the Germans also fired a few smoke shells and the new outfit thought the smoke shells were mustard gas shells. All this must have taken about an hour, before they gave the all clear signal.

About two weeks or so after D-Day, we were given 105 mm short barrel cannons and half-tracks to pull them with. Now we are a full fledged A-1-Cannon Company again. We would advance, dig in, fire the cannons, advance again, dig in and fire the cannons again. But mind you, we were always one or two hills behind the Rifle Companies. If not, I wouldn't be writing this book. I would have probably met my maker many years ago.

Then we stayed set up and firing for about two weeks from the same location.

Then we moved to a new location, but we didn't set up the cannons. The next day, starting about sunrise, all we could hear were huge airplanes and when we looked up the sky was completely covered with huge "V" formations of Allied bombers. There must have been thousands of them. They kept coming for a couple of hours. After they dropped their bombs, they must have circled around and gone back to England for more bombs. This was the beginning of the St. Lo breakthrough in France. We were about seven miles from where the bombs started dropping. The ground was actually shaking where we were, seven miles away. They did what is called saturation bombing. It seems that St. Lo was a big German stronghold where the Germans had regrouped after the D-Day invasion. When the bombing stopped, we got on our half-tracks. Each half-track was pulling a 105 mm cannon and each half-track also had a mounted fifty caliber machine gun on it. I think we also had an Infantry Rifle Company on the half-tracks with us. We were told to ride as fast as we could to St. Lo and when we got there, we were told to ride right through and only stop when we met heavy resistance. We never did meet heavy resistance.

As we got near St. Lo, we could see the huge and unbelievable devastation that the aerial bombings had caused that morning. It was unreal what we saw that day. It was a bright sunny day, and there were huge and I mean huge bomb craters all over the place. The craters were about twenty five to fifty feet apart. They must have dropped five hundred pound bombs or maybe larger bombs. Most of the craters were about ten or fifteen feet deep and about twenty feet in diameter. Maybe deeper and wider. If I remember correctly we didn't go right through St. Lo. We came from the North, and went around the outskirts of town, on the West end.

Other divisions went right into St. Lo to engage the Germans. Everything was in shambles. Very few buildings were standing. When we got on the far side of St. Lo, if I remember correctly, we went about five or ten miles past St. Lo and pulled into a wheat field and set up the cannons.

A few days later we were told that in the fields around St. Lo, the day of the bombing, our Rifle Companies, while going through a few fields saw German soldiers at the far end of the field. As our Infantry advanced through the fields, the German soldiers were looking at our advancing Infantry and they had rifles and machine guns in their hands. But the German soldiers didn't fire their weapons. Our Riflemen kept advancing, but the Germans didn't fire. As our Infantry got real close, they saw that the German soldiers were bleeding out of their mouths, ears and noses. So our Infantry just went right up to the German soldiers and took the rifles and machine guns right out of their hands. We were told that didn't just happen to just a few German soldiers, it happened to numerous German soldiers. They were all taken prisoner. The next day when they were interrogated, they said they saw the American soldiers coming through the fields. The Germans said that they wanted to fire at the advancing American infantry. They tried to fire at our advancing Infantry, but they couldn't. They said, due to the heavy bombing they lost all coordination and they couldn't even pull the triggers on their guns. Our doctors said it was the concussion of the bombs exploding that caused them to bleed from their mouths ears and noses. They had absolutely no coordination of their fingers. They could walk and talk but couldn't control finger movement. I found that a little hard to believe, but about a week or so later, Cannon Company found themselves on the other end of the stick. I will get to that a little later.

A few days after the St. Lo bombing, the rat race began. The idea of the rat race was to bypass the towns and pockets of German soldiers. That way we cut off their supply routes. Then they couldn't get badly needed supplies, such as food, ammunition, gasoline or replacement units. Then our Air Force would bomb and strafe the German soldiers, as they tried to flee East to regroup.

A few nights after the St. Lo breakthrough we were on Cannon Company half-tracks and we had a Rifle Company on the half-tracks with us. As usual, we were told to ride until we met resistance, then stop and fight. Well at first, we were on a main road and after awhile we turned into sort of a side road which was a dirt road through the woods, and there were big trees sort of covering the road. It sort of went up and down small hills. After we rode for about five minutes, we came upon a very eerie scene, first on the right side of the road we saw a German tank parked but nobody was shooting. As we get closer, we saw a German soldier on top of the tank, manning a mounted machine gun. He didn't move or shoot, so our half-tracks slowed down but we didn't shoot and the German didn't shoot either. When we got closer, we could see another German soldier, with his head stuck out of the hatch or turret, whatever you call it. We didn't know if they were dead or just making believe they were dead. So we didn't shoot. Because we were told that we were sneaking through an opening in the German lines, and to be as quiet as possible. We were told not to shoot unless we were shot at. After we passed the first tank, we came to another tank; same thing. One or two soldiers on the outside of the tank. One was sort of lying up against the turret as if he had been shot. As we were riding, we passed about another four tanks. German soldiers either on the tanks, or lying on the ground. We passed all six tanks without incident. It was a narrow dirt road, so as we passed each tank. We were so close that we could have reached out and touched the tanks. To me they didn't look as though they were damaged and the German soldier didn't look dead. I thought we were riding into a trap, so I thought that any minute all hell would break loose; but nothing happened. To this day, I think they were all alive. I think we surprised them and I think they thought we were German vehicles coming up the road, until we got right next to them. Mind you, this was a very narrow twisting road, cut through a forest. Even in daylight, there would be very little visibility. Due to very limited visibility, they didn't realize we were Americans until we were only a few yards from them. They didn't know what to do, so they pretended they were dead. They figured we weren't shooting so they didn't shoot. I think we all had very good guardian angels that night. Next day I told some of the Cannon Company soldiers that I thought those German soldiers were not dead. A few of them said they had the same feeling, that the German soldiers were faking it. Somebody else said it is best to let a sleeping dog sleep.

Maybe they had the same orders that we had that night. Don't make any noise, and don't shoot unless shot at. If so, we all, both sides, should have been given Good Conduct Medals that night.

There is only one thing that I ever did during the war that I am ashamed of. It happened a day or so after passing the German tanks in the woods on the dirt road. Everything was going good. To my way of thinking, it looked like the war would end very soon and I figured any day now, possibly even today, the Germans may surrender. Then I started thinking, it looks like I will survive the war without even being wounded, something which I never really expected.

We moved into a big wheat field about midnight and dug the cannons in, then we all dug fox holes, and went to sleep except those on guard duty. The next morning, it was a beautiful, bright sunny day. About 10:00 AM, we were all sitting around the fox holes and gun pits, talking and having coffee. Everything was nice and quiet. Then all of a sudden we all heard a large artillery shell coming at us. We all hit the ground. Then I heard what I hated to hear. A few of our guys were hollering "Medic". Whenever I heard them holler "Medic", I always felt like I was going to have a heart attack. Especially today, because I figured the war could possibly end today. So I grabbed my medical kit and charged to one of the gun pits where a few of the guys were waving. As I arrived there, two other Cannon Company medics arrived at the same time. I had more experience than them, because I had been in Africa and Sicily. Therefore, I should have taken over. There was only one soldier wounded from that artillery shell that had just exploded, but he was very badly wounded. He had a big hole about the size of my mess kit up high on his back left side, just behind the heart. He wasn't bleeding too much, but a big piece of flesh was missing. Normally, I would have taken over, and not considered my personal safety. But being that I had this gut feeling, that the Germans were beaten, and they would surrender any day, possibly even today, I became extra cautious and protective of myself. I sure as hell didn't want to get my ass shot off the last day of the war. Knowing that it was a large artillery shell that had just exploded, I figured being that it was only one artillery shell that they fired, I figured the German artillery observer had us under direct observation, and that shot was fired for him to get our range, and with that shot exploding right in front of our center cannon. I figured he was zeroed in on us perfectly. I figured any second a whole battery of German cannons would be shelling our position for the next ten or fifteen minutes. If so, the best place to be would be in a deep fox hole. So now in a split second I had to decide what to do. I chose the cowards way out. When the cannon was dug in, as usual a small low trench is dug only about a foot deep at the rear of the cannon and the earth that is dug out of the trench is piled up in front of the cannon, for protection against incoming artillery or mortar shells. So we three medics arrived there at about the same time. The wounded soldier was lying face down, out in front and on top of the two foot high pile of dirt that was put there, when the trench for the cannon was dug. So instead of me running right to the wounded soldier, I jumped into the gunpit and told one of the other new medics that this would be a good time for him to learn what to do. So I stayed in the relative safety of the one foot deep trench and handed him morphine, sulpha powder and huge bandages to put on the wound. I was a real coward that day. I was hiding in the one foot deep trench while he was up on top of a pile of dirt doing my job. Incidentally, no more shells came into our area that day. The wounded soldier was put on a stretcher and taken by jeep to the First Aid station. When the doctor examined him, he was pronounced dead on arrival. Nobody ever criticized me for my actions that day. But I know I was a coward that day. But I must say, that to my knowledge that was the only time that I was ever a coward during the war. Most of the time I lived up to the First Division Motto, which is, "No Mission Too Difficult, No Sacrifice Too Great, Duty First." I know the only reason I didn't jump right in and do my job that day, was because of that crazy feeling I had that day, that I thought the Germans would surrender and the war would be over, and I didn't want to be killed or wounded that last day of the war.

A day or so later, I adapted my old way of looking at things. I convinced myself that it is still going to be a long war, and I would probably be killed before the war ends. And also that my mother would collect my ten thousand dollar insurance policy, and everything would be okay.

So about a week and a half later, I got a chance to redeem myself. We were at different location, all dug in, and firing the cannons like mad, both day and night. Then one day Captain O'Brien called all the Sergeants and Corporals together and said that he needed one cannon and crew to volunteer for a very risky assignment. He said the Rifle Companies were dug in down the road about a half mile in front of us, and early every evening for the last three days, a German tank would appear over a small hill, and shell the hell out of the Rifle Companies direct fire for about fifteen minutes and then take off like a bat out of hell, and disappear back over the same hill. But in that time he caused a lot of casualties with our Rifle Companies. Now Captain O'Brien said it will be a very dangerous mission and said the German tank shows up about the same time early every evening. He said I only want one cannon and one crew to volunteer. He said, "This is what you will be volunteering for. We need one half-track to pull the cannon. The half-track will be loaded with armor piercing shells, and about an hour before the German tank is expected to appear, the volunteer crew will go to the location and set up the cannon and have a whole bunch of rounds of armor piercing shells lying on the ground right next to the cannon for rapid firing. And remember, you will be swapping shots, direct fire with a tank. You will have absolutely no protection. It is also possible that more than one tank will appear." So enough men and a half-track driver volunteered to form a full crew. When the crew was assembled, the Sergeant in charge asked about a medic. Captain O'Brien said "No medic." When I heard no medic, I went to the volunteer crew and told them that I wanted to go with them. They all said okay. So we devised a plan. "As the half-track pulling the cannon leaves the field to get onto the dirt road, to stop for a minute, and I will be hiding there in the bushes, with extra medical supplies." They stopped as planned. I handed up my big wooden box of medical supplies and then I climbed on board. What we didn't expect was that most of Cannon Company soldiers were mulling around at that end of the field to watch us leave. I think that almost everybody in Cannon Company saw the half-track stop and pick me up. Nobody said anything. They waved at us and we waved at them.

Well, when we arrived at our planned location one, two, three, like clock work, we all jumped off the half-track, unhooked the cannon, set it up, loaded it and ready to fire, all in about two minutes. We never dug the cannon in, we had to be ready to fire immediately. Just in case the German tank showed up early. We never dug fox holes, we had to be alert and ready to fire. We waited and waited, but the German tank never showed up. We waited until just before dark then we left. We don't know if the German tank left the area before we got there, or if he saw us and just didn't want to swap shots. Why he never showed up, we never found out. But it didn't really make any of us angry. When we got back we rejoined the rest of Cannon Company. They all came over and asked what happened.

That's the way it is in combat, one day nothing bothers you, and the next day, you want to crawl into a hole and hide. As they say "Such is war." I would like to also add very unpredictable.

Now I will tell you what happened to Cannon Company one night. We were on the move one beautiful moonlit night and there was a big full moon, not a cloud in the sky, absolutely beautiful. We were in a small convoy, moving from one location to another. We had Rifle Company soldiers on the half-tracks with us. Cannon Company half-tracks were leading the convoy. I was in about the fourth half-track from the front of the convoy. The orders were, ride until we met opposition, then stop and fight. We went about five miles enjoying looking at the big full moon. Then we came to hill country, and went up a big hill or it could have been called a small mountain. It was a single lane, paved road. We were driving along the top of the hills, when we heard a plane, it kept circling back and forth from one end of the convoy to the other. It was a dense woods where we were, big trees were overhanging and covering a lot of the road. The convoy stopped and waited to see what was going to happen. We all kept very still, hoping he wouldn't see us. After awhile, about four more planes joined him. Then they dropped flares all over the place. Between the bright moon and the flares it was like broad daylight. I believe the road was running East and West. Then they all went off to the West. All of a sudden, they all turned and came right at us, bombing and strafing and dropping more flares. Then they would turn and pass a little North of us, I guess so we couldn't get a good shot at them. When they got a little West of us they would turn and come right at us again, bombing and strafing as they flew over us, also dropping more flares. But this time, a lot of our guys mounted the fifty caliber machine guns and fired at them. After about three or four runs over us, bombing and strafing they must have run out of ammunition. So all but one of them left. The one that stayed, kept circling and dropping flares. About ten minutes later, three or four more came back. And they did the same thing until they ran out of ammunition again. Again, one stayed and the rest left. The one that stayed kept circling and every now and then dropping flares. This went on for well over an hour. Finally they all left.

Now I'll tell you what happened to me during this fracas. At first, when the single plane was just circling overhead we stopped the convoy, because it was a wooded area and we were partly under big trees. We were hoping the guy in the plane wouldn't see us. So we just sat on the half-tracks. But when his friends showed up, and started dropping flares, we still just sat on the half-tracks without moving, still hoping they wouldn't see us. But when they started strafing and bombing we knew the half-tracks weren't a very safe place, so we all jumped off and ran into the woods on the South side of the road. Somebody hollered, "Over here, there's a gully here." So I ran that way and dove into the gully. The gully seemed to run from the road way back into the woods. The gully was deep, it was over my head. There were about five or six of us in the gully. We called and told others about the gully and after awhile some more jumped into the gully. I figured the gully was about the safest place around. Every time the planes came over, and dropped their bombs the ground would shimmer and a shower of dirt, rocks and tree branches would fall all over us. I figured I was in a good safe place but then I started praying that nobody else would get hit. If someone was hit, someone would holler, "Medic" and I would have to leave my safe haven and go to administer first aid. After awhile I realized that it appeared that they weren't bombing and strafing the road. They seemed to be bombing and strafing in the woods, where we were. You could hear some of our soldiers still firing the fifty caliber machine guns at the German planes. That may be the reason they were bombing and strafing in the woods, so as to avoid giving our guys manning the machine guns a good shot at them. Also possibly, that the big trees were covering the road, and they weren't sure where the road was. Anyhow, I carried a German bayonet attached to my belt. At first I was okay nice and calm. But when the bombs kept falling, I took out the German bayonet and dug a hole in the wall of the gully. And every time I heard the bombs whistling down, I would stick my head in the hole. Not that it would help but I guess for survival people will try anything. I know, every time I heard the bombs whistling down and I stuck my head in the hole, I did feel safer. The bombing went on for over an hour. After we were in the gully for about forty-five minutes. One of the soldiers in the gully called me and said "George, do you have the German bayonet with you?" I said, "Yes, why do you want it?" He said, "I want to dig a hole, to stick my head in." I told him, "Yes," and when he came over near me, I tried to unhook the bayonet from my belt. But I couldn't unhook it, I had no coordination with my fingers. I told him, and he laughed and said he would unhook it. But he couldn't do it either. He said he also lost coordination with his fingers. Then I remembered about the German soldiers and how they lost all coordination of their fingers at the St. Lo bombing. They couldn't pull the triggers on their rifles. Now I believe the St. Lo story about lost coordination.

Anyway, after about an hour or so, the planes left. We were given orders to mount up and get the hell out of there, before the planes returned. When we returned to the road, we were surprised to see that none of the front vehicles were damaged. So we hopped on the half-tracks and got the hell out of there. I don't really know what happened to the center or rear of the convoy.

We were kind of jumpy for the remainder of the night, and the next day.

As we moved on the next day or so, we came upon some bombed out German convoys. Some were all tank convoys. Some were half-truck and half-tank convoys. In the beginning, the German bombed out convoys were all vehicle convoys. But as we advanced further East, I guess the Germans were running out of gasoline, because every now and then we would find horse-drawn, knocked out German convoys. If we had time we would do a little looting of the German knocked out convoys.

One horse-drawn convoy we came upon had covered wagons like I used to see in the movies, like the pioneers used going out West in the 1800's. It was still on fire when we got there, so I did a little scouting. On one of the covered wagons I found a bunch of big thin wooden boxes which looked like very big brief cases. They were about three feet high and about three feet wide, and only about three inches thick. Most of them were completely burnt out. But I did find one that was only partly burnt so I opened it up. It was full of brand new German paper money. It must have been a German soldiers payroll vehicle. The bills were about 95% burnt. I found a few that were only partly burnt or not burnt at all. These I put in my pocket. Later, when the war ended I was able to use them in German taverns.

Another time, we came upon another burnt out horse-drawn German convoy. One of the covered wagons was loaded with boxes so I opened one of the boxes. What a pleasant surprise, it was loaded with small cans of crabmeat. I sat there about twenty minutes opening and eating one can after the other. All good First Division soldiers always carried a cork-screw, a can-opener and a knife. Then it was time to leave, so I filled my pockets and inside my shirt, with as many cans as I could carry. When I told the other soldiers where I found the crabmeat, a few of them ran back and took as many as they could carry. I think the labels on the cans said they were from Norway. They were delicious, they were probably German officers rations. I often wonder if they had it shipped from Norway, or if they stole it in Norway. Oh well, as they say, "All's Fair in Love and War." No matter how it got there, I was glad it was there. And I said thanks to the dive bomber pilots who knocked that convoy out.

Another time, when we were driving through France we stopped on the South side of the road, and it was a very nice peaceful looking place. On the North side of the road, there was some kind of a big fence or wall about seven feet high. It seemed to be a very large closed-in area. At the South East end of the wall, was a driveway and a huge fancy gate. There was some kind of old plaque on the left side of the gate. I thought it must have been an enclosed and secluded mansion, so I walked across the street and read the plaque. Some of the other soldiers asked what it said. I started to laugh, and answered, "You will never believe what it says. Then I told them, "It says, this is an American Soldier's Cemetery from World War One." Everybody laughed, and one soldier looked up at the sky waved and said "How is it up there fellows?" We all laughed. Then it was time to get on the half-tracks and we left. I think as we left we all looked back. Now we were all sort of on the silent side.

It was around that time that the American, English and Canadian armies, closed what was called the Falaise pocket. It was sort of a flanking movement. The American, English and Canadian. Armies formed a huge circle around the German Army. That maneuver cut off all supply lines leading into the surrounded German army. There was fighting back and forth. I think the way it ended, most of the Germans surrendered.

I remember one day Cannon Company was set up in a holding position. There was some shelling back and forth. Then all of a sudden we heard something that sounded like a freight train, coming through the air. We could tell it was coming right at us. We all hit the dirt, but the thing never exploded. It hit the ground right near us so nobody moved for about five minutes, maybe longer. We thought maybe it had a delayed action fuse. But there never was an explosion. When we located it, there was a deep hole in the ground, we don't know how deep the hole was. The hole was about a foot and a half in diameter. We figured it must have been one of those big railroad guns. When we looked in the hole, we couldn't see anything. It must have weighed a ton and went way down deep in the ground. So we roped off that area. Then we moved two of our cannons to a safer location. Nobody ever went near that hole again. We stayed at that location for another day. We were all glad when we were told to pack up and move on.

While moving through France, everything was going good but then one day Captain O'Brien of Cannon Company assembled the company together in a big open field. He said, "We have a very serious problem that must be solved immediately." He told us that for a few days now, whenever we fired the cannons all the rounds are falling very short of where they should be falling. He asked us if anybody knew why the rounds keep falling short. Nobody could figure out why the rounds should be falling short. He said there has to be an explanation and we must figure out what the reason is. He said he wanted to hear from anyone, not only the Sergeants and Corporals. He said he wanted to hear from the P.F.C.s and Privates, anyone who thinks they might know something no matter how ridiculous it may seem. Nobody knew the answer. Then he said that there has to be an answer, "Does anybody have an answer, no matter how crazy it may sound." At that point a new Private raised his hand and said he noticed something different for a few days now. Captain O'Brien said, "Okay now relax, don't be ashamed, let us know anything that you think pertains to this." The Private said, "You know how we put sticks in a clearing, to build a little fire to heat our c-rations or cook coffee, then next we sprinkle gun powder, from the powder charge bags from the cannon all around and into the little pile of sticks and then make a small trail of gunpowder a few feet away from the pile of sticks. And then we light the small trail of gunpowder which in turn travels to the pile of little sticks and it then sets the sticks on fire to cook our food or coffee. At that point, everybody laughed. Captain O'Brien told everybody to shut up. Then he said, "I know how we build small fires for cooking, but what does that have to do with our artillery shells falling short?" Captain O'Brien said, "Keep talking. I think you know something and you are about to tell us." So the Private said, "When we cut open the powder charge cloth bags to sprinkle the gun powder on the ground to build our fires for cooking, I noticed for the last few days the powder granules are a different size and shape from what they used to be." Captain O'Brien said, "That's it. You are right, remember a few days ago, we ran out of ammunition for our 105 mm short barrel cannons. We had to settle for 105 mm long barrel cannon ammunition." He said, "That's around the time the rounds started falling short."

He said, "Get me a field artillery manual. He looked it up and said, "That's the problem. Just as the Private said. There is definitely a difference in the powder charges. We can use the ammunition from the long barrel 105 mm howitzers. But we have to change the elevation settings on our cannons when firing." Captain O'Brien went right back to the O.P. (Observation Post) and picked out an enemy target and tested each cannon. Everything was perfect from then on. We just had to be careful checking the powder charges. I don't remember, but I guess Captain O'Brien promoted the Private to a P.F.C. or something.

One night, while going through France, we pulled into a big wheat field and dug in. There were very old and very big trees all around the edges of the wheat field. About 5:00 AM we were told to line up and stand at attention. At that time, the war was going good for us. The Germans were in full retreat. We were chasing them from town to town. We were moving far and fast everyday. So when we lined up that morning we were told that we had to slow down for a day or so to wait for supplies to catch up to us. So Cannon Company First Sergeant Harold, his nick name was Sergeant China, he was a Regular Army career soldier, he had about eighteen years in the Army at that time. The reason they called him Sergeant China, I was told, was because before the war he was stationed someplace in China as an American soldier for about four years. I don't know where or why he was stationed in China. Maybe with an American Embassy or something like that. I was also told that when he got drunk he would talk in Chinese. I never heard him, but that's what I was told. So now, to get back to us standing at attention that bright sunny day in the middle of this big wheat field. Sergeant Harold or Sergeant China, or whatever you want to call him, told us that he was proud of us on D-Day and every day after that. He told us that we deserved a break. He said that he believes that when it is time to work, everybody works. And when its is time to play everybody plays. He said that we will be at this location for a day or so. He then said that this is our rest area for a day or so. He looked at his watch and said, "It is now 5:30 AM and by noon time I want you all to be so drunk, that you can climb the tallest trees and jump off head first and not get hurt. So we had a merry old time that day. Most of us spent the next day trying to sober up. The day after that we started chasing the German Army again.

For the next few weeks, as we advanced we would come upon several more German convoys that were completely bombed out, set afire, and strafed by our Air Force. Most of the damage was caused by our dive bombers. When they caught a German convoy on the road, our planes would first bomb the front of the convoy and then they would bomb the rear of the convoy. That way, with the first couple of trucks or tanks knocked out and the last couple of trucks or tanks knocked out, the remainder of the convoy was trapped in the middle, and had no place to go. Then our planes would just keep flying back and forth, bombing and strafing until all vehicles were set afire. I must say, our planes did a terrific job spotting and destroying German convoys, both day and night. In the night time, if our planes spotted any movement on the ground, they would drop flares and if it turned out to be a German convoy, our planes wouldn't leave until the convoy was completely destroyed. The Germans mainly moved on small back roads after dark, hoping our planes wouldn't find them.

While chasing the Germans through France one hot sunny day, we were riding on Cannon Company half-tracks. We also had a Rifle Company riding on the half-tracks with us. The orders were the same, ride until we get shot at then dismount and fight. We must have been riding about an hour, when our convoy stopped. It was a routine stop in case anybody had to relieve themselves. I was in about the third half-track from the front of the convoy. Where we stopped, there was a gradual long curve in the road. There was tall grass or weeds on both sides of the road, the weeds were about two and a half feet tall. I got off on the right side of the road. On the side I got off the ground sloped up. The tall grass and weeds went gradually up the slope for about a hundred yards. Past that was a very dark and dense woods. When I got off I started to walk into the tall weeds up the slope towards the woods. As I walked along towards the woods, I passed a few dead German soldiers lying on the ground in the tall grass. I couldn't see them until I got real close to them. They were all sort of scattered out, not close to each other, then I stopped and relieved myself. When finished I sort of walked a little closer up the slope towards the woods and there I saw a German officer lying on the ground face down, his left hand under his forehead and his right hand under his stomach. At first I was going to roll him over and take his field glasses and luger. But as I got closer I stopped. He didn't look wounded and he looked too fresh and clean to be dead. I figured maybe he and his friends weren't dead. I figured maybe they were hiding in the woods and tall weeds watching us coming up the road. But they didn't expect us to stop, dismount and walk into the tall weeds to relieve ourselves. So when they saw us stop and walk into the tall grass, they had three choices. #1 -Surrender. #2 - Start shooting, I don't know how many of them were hiding in the woods and tall weeds. But we had a good size convoy, there must have been five or six hundred of us maybe more. So I think they made a good choice by not shooting. #3 Hit the dirt and play dead. So there I am about four feet from this German officer, who was lying on the ground. I didn't have a pistol with me at that time. I could see his field glasses but I couldn't see his luger. Then I figured he might be holding it in his right hand, under his stomach. I figured if I roll him over and he is dead I can take his field glasses and his Luger. But then I figured if he is alive he will get to keep his field glasses and his Luger, and the only thing I would get was a few bullets in my tummy. So I figured awe, what the heck, it is his pistol and his field glasses. Let him keep them. So I went back to the half-track and climbed aboard. Nobody said anything so I didn't say anything either. So away we went down the road, still searching for the retreating German Army. After all, some say survival is the name of the game.

As we were riding along on the half-tracks after leaving there, I started to wonder about those German soldiers lying on the ground. Then it dawned on me that they had to be alive. There were no holes in the ground where bombs or artillery shells had exploded. Also, we were the first Allied

The Way I Remember It

soldiers to go into that area. No other Allied soldiers ever went down that road. So I guess they had to be alive. Then I figured we are having a nice quiet, peaceful ride enjoying the French countryside. So I shut up, sat back and enjoyed the ride.

We passed Paris on the South side. I could see the Eiffel Tower in the distance. Then we headed sort of Northeast towards Belgium. I don't remember too much about the journey from South of Paris to Belgium. The First Division had some skirmishes and took a lot of prisoners between Paris and Belgium. Going through France, we moved so far and so fast almost every day. After awhile I just stopped looking at the names of the towns. Sometimes we would pass through three, four or more towns a day. It just didn't matter to me where we were, or where we were going. I figured, eventually I would probably get killed, and my mother would get $10,000 and that would probably make the whole thing worth while.

CHAPTER SEVEN:

BELGIUM

As we entered the Belgium towns, the people were very friendly. But what amazed me the most was how clean the towns were. The streets and stoops of the houses looked like they were swept and hosed every day. It looked the same as American towns looked before World War Two, not the way American towns look today. Dirty, sloppy, filthy, graffiti, painting all over the apartment houses, subway trains, bridges, fences, directional signs on the highways, you name it, anything to show ignorance and stupidity. I think the words neatness and cleanliness should be removed from the American Dictionary. They have very little meaning to the American population today. Blame whoever you want, I blame the parents and the parents alone.

We entered Belgium near Mons. We pulled into a small park which was across the street from apartment houses. Everything was so nice, neat and clean and the apartment houses were very cheerful looking. I believe they were made of white or light gray bricks, if I remember correctly. The cannons were dug in and set up in the park, and for some reason we didn't dig fox holes, because we were told we could sleep in the cellar of the apartment houses which we did. The Germans were in mass retreat at that time, trying to get back into Germany. I guess that is why we didn't dig fox holes. Well anyway, those on guard duty stayed in the park, minding the cannons. Those not on guard duty were sleeping in the basement of one of the apartment houses, including me. Well, the way I remember, it must have been about 2:00 AM. For some reason, I woke up and heard soldiers marching outside in the street, or on the sidewalk. I thought they must have been German soldiers and I figured any minute all hell would break loose. It sounded like a couple of hundred soldiers marching. But nothing ever happened. In the morning I didn't mention it and nobody else ever mentioned it. To this day, I don't know who marched past that night.

Then about twenty five years after the war ended, I read someplace, I don't remember where, an article which said that in World War One some very strange things happened in Mons. I don't know if the article was true or not. So I won't write about it here. But every now and then, I think about it.

CHAPTER EIGHT:

GERMANY

After Mons, we worked our way towards the Seigfried Line and into our first German towns near Aachen. It took about a month of very severe fighting, before the town of Aachen surrendered. Our Rifle Companies had to fight street by street, house by house and even room by room, capturing or killing all the defending German soldiers. Before a German general finally surrendered the town of Aachen, there were a lot of casualties on both sides.

During the battle of Aachen, Cannon Company was firing cannons into Aachen both day and night. We changed location a few times that month or so, but no matter where the cannons were set up, Aachen was the main target twenty four hours a day. I remember one field we moved into and set up the cannons. We were on low land and in the distance we could see some fairly high hills. I didn't like that location, because if the German soldiers were on those hills, we would be under direct observation. We stayed there about four or five days. We were continuously shelling Aachen and those hills and low land in front of the hills. Every now and then the Germans would shell Cannon Company. When they shelled us we would jump into our fox holes, which were right near the cannons. When their barrage showed up, we would jump out of our fox holes and Cannon Company would shell the German positions. I remember one bright, sunny day we were sitting around the cannons laughing and joking, when all of a sudden the Germans started shelling Cannon Company. The shells were exploding all around our gun emplacements. When I heard the first shells coming in, I hit the dirt right next to one of our cannons. When I hit the dirt, my helmet hit a piece of metal. After the shell exploded, I raised my head to see what the metal was that my helmet had hit. When I raised my head, I was looking into the face of another Cannon Company soldier. We looked at each other and started to laugh. It seems that when the shells started coming in, we both hit the ground at the same time and we landed helmet to helmet. We both stayed there for a while as more shells kept coming in. After a while the shells were getting closer and closer. We both had fox holes only about twenty feet away from where we were lying. As the shells kept getting closer and closer, I finally said to the other soldier, Private Van Ought, "This is getting too close for comfort. I am going to run and jump into my fox hole. And I think you should do the same thing." He laughed and said, "No this is okay." After the next round of shells exploded, I jumped up and started towards my fox hole. All of a sudden I heard another round of shells coming in. I could tell one was real close, so I dove head first into my fox hole. As I hit the bottom of my fox hole, the shell exploded and kicked a lot of rocks and dirt into my fox hole. I didn't hear any more shells coming in, so I stood up in my fox hole, and saw the shell had exploded right where I had been lying on the ground. I jumped out of my fox hole and ran to see how Van Ought was. When I picked him up by the shoulders I saw that he was split in two, from the chest down. A little later I heard more shells coming in, so I jumped back into my fox hole. I said a prayer for Van Ought. And I guess, for myself, but I don't remember if I said one for myself. I probably did but I am not sure. I think that night we left that location and went to another field and dug the cannons in and started firing at Aachen again.

This time we were in a small valley, and there was a creek running along one side of the valley, sort of like a babbling brook. It was a very pretty location. There was a cluster of small farm buildings at one end of the valley, where most of the cannons were set up. I dug my fox hole away from the farm buildings. I figured the buildings would be a target for our planes and German planes, and also a target for German artillery and mortars. We stayed there for about two weeks, shooting at Aachen and various other targets. One night I went into my fox hole, I must have slept like a baby, I didn't hear anything. When I woke up, it must have been about 5:00 AM. I was hungry, so I went towards the farm buildings to get something to eat. Everybody was talking about what had happened about 2:00 AM and I didn't know anything had happened. They told me a German plane came over and dropped flares and came in strafing and bombing. He got a direct hit in one of the gun pits, knocking out and flipping a cannon upside down, but most of us were sleeping and nobody got hit.

While we were at that location a funny thing happened. The German farmers and their families were very friendly. When they realized we were also friendly and weren't going to harm them, they became more relaxed and more friendly. There was a German farmer about thirty years old. He was well built and very strong looking. The first couple of days he kept to himself and just did his farm work. He would give us a friendly nod, but he wouldn't speak to us. After a few days, he would speak to us and we would speak to him. Then one day one of our guys asked if he could get us something to drink. He laughed and said "Okay." A little later he returned with a couple of bottles of wine. After that, we all became good friends. We stayed there about two weeks, and every now and then he would get us more wine. One of our guys had a camera and took some pictures of us with him. I still have one of he and I and a few other Cannon Company soldiers standing, posing and smiling with our hands on each other's shoulders.

George A. Flynn

After about two weeks, we told him we were going to move out the next day. So early the next morning we were getting ready to leave, when all of a sudden he showed up with a German soldier's uniform on. He held his hands up and said he surrendered. We told him that he didn't have to hold his hands up and we all had a good laugh. He said he was proud to surrender to the First Infantry Division. The kitchen was set up and it was chow time. Our Officers told him to have chow with us before they put him on a jeep and sent him to the rear. Before he left, we all shook hands. He wished us good luck, and we wished him good luck. He told us that the farm was actually his home. He said he was home on leave to visit his mother and father when we showed up, and he didn't know what to do, so he just took off his uniform and put on his civilian clothes and just started helping his father working on the farm. When he saw how friendly we were, he decided to surrender to us.

Everyday is a new story, a new adventure, some pleasant, some not so pleasant. After awhile you just seem to take everything in stride. After awhile you just don't seem to care what happens. You just keep going from day to day. I think all combat soldiers, after awhile, adapt the old saying, "What is to be shall be." Also "Live and be Merry, for tomorrow you may be dead."

A couple of months before the war ended, the American Army came out with what was called the point system. What the point system was, was when a soldier got a certain number of points, he can be sent back to the States and doesn't have to see anymore combat unless he chooses to see more combat. If he wants to stay in the Army, he can stay in the Army. And if he chooses to leave the Army, he may leave the Army.

I think the point system started around the beginning of December 1944, about two weeks before the Battle of the Bulge started. The point system went something like this. A soldier would get a few points for every month in combat and he would also get a few points for every Battle Star he wears on his Campaign Ribbon. The most Battle Stars given out in the European theater of operations was eight Battle Stars. I ended up with seven Battle Stars. Also on the same campaign ribbon, a soldier would wear an arrow spearhead for each D-Day invasion he made. The old soldiers of the First Infantry Division wore three Arrow Heads on their campaign ribbons. I wore two Arrowheads because I was a rookie. Next with the point system, a few points were given if you were wounded in combat, and wore a Purple Heart medal. Some First Division Rifle Company soldiers were wounded three or four times, maybe more. Thank the Lord I was never wounded. Cannon Company was usually one or two hills behind the Rifle Companies. Next, a soldier was given a few points for each decoration he received in combat, such as a Bronze or Silver Star, or any other higher medals he may have received in combat. Well when the point system started, all that was needed was about seventy five or eighty points to be sent back to the States, which meant almost every old regular army soldier of the First Division, could have been sent back to the States. They all had well over a hundred points. I think about 95% of them volunteered to stay until the war ended. When the war ended, most of the old regular army First Division soldiers ended up with about a hundred and forty or a hundred and fifty points. I think I ended up with about a hundred and fifteen points.

After Aachen I don't remember exactly where we went or what we did. But on December 16, 1944 the Battle of the Bulge started.

CHAPTER NINE:

BATTLE OF THE BULGE

The First Infantry Division was on line since making the D-Day landing at Normandy France on June 6, 1944.

About two weeks before Christmas 1944, they pulled us off line and we were sent to the rear for a rest. We pulled into this fair sized Belgium town of ? Sorry I can't remember the name of the town.

I was still with Cannon Company and we were naturally riding half-tracks which were pulling the cannons. The half-tracks stopped in the center of town. Cannon Company soldiers were told to take all their small arms, such as rifles, pistols and ammunition for such, and line up down the block in front of a big hotel which was to be our home, until it was time for us to go back on line. I told the Cannon Company soldiers on my half-track that I was going to stay on the half-track. Because they all knew that I had a beautiful Belgium pistol that I had taken off a dead German soldier. It was a beautiful thirty eight that fired about sixteen rounds without reloading. I carried it in a shoulder holster under my shirt because a medic was not supposed to carry fire arms. They all knew I loved it, and wanted to take it home after the war ended which I did. So they all said okay and they would cover for me, which they did. At roll call when my name was called they said I had diarrhea and had to run to the toilet. Everybody laughed, but nobody checked. So when they all got off the half-track and lined up for roll call and inspection they had to turn in their rifles, pistols, and ammunition because we were in a rest area and they didn't want us roaming the streets with firearms. While this was going on, I was lying down on the floor of the half-track. Every now and then I would kneel up and peek, they were about four hundred feet from the half-track all standing at attention, so I lay down on the floor of the half-track again. While lying down, I started to look around at the houses, and to my surprise there was a very pretty lady looking out of the second floor window of the house that we were parked in front of. I smiled at her and she smiled at me. I waved at her and she waved at me. I knew she was wondering why I didn't get off the half-track and line up with the other soldiers. So I reached into my pocket and pulled out my Red Cross Arm Band. I showed it to her. Then I reached into my shoulder holster and showed her my pistol. Then I showed her a wooden German soldier's ammunition box, which I used to carry my medical supplies. I took out some bandages and other medical supplies and showed it to her. Then we both started to use sign language. Through sign language I explained that if the officers saw my pistol, I would have to turn it in and because I was a medic they probably wouldn't give it back to me. I knew she understood what I was saying. Next, she pointed to a wooden door about fifty feet away from her front door. She motioned for me to jump off the half-track and run to the wooden door. She then motioned for me to bring the pistol. Then she motioned for me to wait until she got downstairs and opened the wooden door. I motioned okay. We both smiled and laughed. I waited a few minutes, then peeked over the top of the half-track. She was standing there with the wooden door open. Cannon Company was still lined up at attention about four hundred feet away. When nobody from Cannon Company was looking towards the half-tracks, I jumped off and ran to the wooden door. When I entered the wooden door I found myself in some kind of a huge courtyard. I think it had a cobblestone floor. When I entered into the courtyard, she closed and locked the wooden door and was very friendly and showed me around the courtyard. We communicated mostly by sign language and the very little French I could speak. She took me upstairs to her apartment and I think she gave me a glass of wine. Her apartment was very nice and neat. Then she showed me her baby, who appeared to be only a few months old. We sat at the kitchen table and talked about the war. After awhile we heard a commotion outside. She called me to the front window. Cannon Company soldiers were getting their packs off the half-tracks so I asked if I could leave my pistol with her. She said, "okay" and put it in a dresser drawer and told me she would leave it there with my ammo. I thanked her and told her I had to leave. She walked me down to the wooden door. On the way down she told me if I had any soiled clothes that needed washing to bring them to her and she would have them cleaned for me. She said don't tell the other soldiers. She told me when I came back to ring the front bell and stand out where she could see me. And then she would come down and open the wooden door to the courtyard. I said "Okay." I kissed her on the hand and left.

Then I went down the block to the big hotel where we were to stay. We all cleaned up, took clean clothes out of our packs.

Then Cannon Company kitchen crew cooked us a hot meal. Then we were told that we could walk around the town. But we were told there was a 10:00 PM curfew. If we weren't back by 10:00 PM we would be punished by extra duty and not allowed out for a full week. So we left and went walking around town and there were some taverns, so naturally, that is where most of us ended up. I made sure I was back before 10:00 PM.

Next day was clean up day. We all cleaned the half-tracks and cannons. Now we have the prettiest cannons and half-tracks in Europe.

That afternoon I put my soiled clothes in a paper bag, and went and rang the front door bell and then stood out by the curb so the pretty lady could see me. A few minutes later the wooden door opened and there was that same smiling pretty lady. She invited me in and I told her I had a bag of soiled clothes. She took the bag and put it in a laundry room at the far end of the courtyard. She invited me upstairs. We had coffee, and sat and talked for a couple of hours. She told me her husband was out of town, and wouldn't be back for a week or so. About 9:00 PM I told her about the curfew and explained that I had to be back by 10:00 PM. We both laughed about the curfew. About 9:30 I left. She told me I could come back whenever I wanted to.

The next afternoon I called on her again. I asked if she wanted to go to a restaurant or a tavern for a few drinks. She said she would like that but she couldn't because it was a small town and no matter where we went people would know her, and if she was seen with an American soldier, the whole town would know and it would get back to her husband. I said I understood. So she invited me up to her apartment again. I said yes, I would love to go upstairs again. So that is the way it was for my stay in that town, which lasted only a few days. The rumor was that we would be in this town for about a month because this was to be our rest area. But we were only there a few days because the German army made a major offensive attack. They broke through the American lines on a massive scale. This is what became known as the "Battle of The Bulge." They broke through the

American lines with tanks and infantry and they were heading to capture the major American ammunition and gasoline storage areas, which they desperately needed.

The weather favored the German breakthrough. The weather was very cloudy, and very low hanging clouds and sort of foggy weather. Which meant that the German tanks and trucks could use the main roads without being bombed and strafed, and they took full advantage of the weather. You could say they moved like a bat out of hell racing for the American gas and ammo dumps. Because of the weather, our Air Force had to stay on the ground for about four or five days.

The German attack came as a complete surprise. You might say the Germans caught the American Army with their pants down.

Now to get back to Cannon Company 16$^{\underline{th}}$ Infantry Regiment of the First Infantry Division of which I was part. Well as I said earlier, we thought we were going to stay about a month in this beautiful Belgium town, which was to be our rest area. But we were only there a few days when the German Army broke through the American lines, which was the beginning of the "Battle of the Bulge". So we were told we were going back on line, which meant we were only in that Belgium town for about three days. When I heard we were going back on line, I ran down the block and rang the bell near the wooden door. When I rang the bell, I looked up and saw that very pretty lady leaning out the window and waving at me. She looked very frightened and worried and signaled for me to wait, that she would be right down. A few minutes later, the wooden door opened and she invited me into the courtyard. She then locked the wooden door. We stood looking at each other, she had tears in her eyes. We held hands for a minute or two just looking at each other. Then we hugged and kissed a few times and she invited me upstairs. We sat at the kitchen table and talked mostly using sign language. After awhile she took out a bottle of wine and we sat and talked some more. She had been listening to the radio and knew that the Germans had pierced the American front lines and they were on a rampage. She was worried that the Germans would come back into this town, and said a lot of people were starting to leave town. They were afraid because we were there and if the Germans came back, they were afraid they would be caught in the middle of a battle zone. They were afraid the artillery would start shelling the town and if the Germans got into the town the American planes would start bombing the town. And I knew that what she was saying could actually happen, but I couldn't tell her that because she was very upset. I then told her I had to leave. I told her that we had to get back on the half-tracks and go back on line. She really started crying then. She ran into another room and came back with my clean clothes, pistol, shoulder holster and ammo. I put the shoulder holster and pistol on under my shirt, and then took my clean clothes and told her that I really had to leave. She said she understood and told me to write a letter. I said, "Yes." We both went downstairs into the courtyard and when we got to the wooden door, she said a prayer and sort of blessed me. She told me to come back if possible. I said, "Yes." We then hugged and gave each other a beautiful long kiss. She opened the door and I left.

Cannon Company was starting to load onto the half-tracks so I ran down the block to the hotel, got my pack and ran back to the half-track. I then got on the half-track. The Cannon Company soldiers asked where I had been and I told them I had been in Heaven for a few days. They all laughed. A little while later, the half-tracks started to move. It was early evening, and as we passed her house, I looked up and she was leaning out the window. We both waved at each other. I threw her a kiss and she threw me a kiss. That was the last time I ever saw that very beautiful lady.

As the half-tracks moved around in and out of various streets, every time we stopped, people would come running up to the half-tracks and give us bottles of wine and Cognac. There was mass confusion throughout the town. People were loading cars, trucks, pushcarts and wagons with their personal belongings, blankets, clothes, food and whatever they could carry. It seemed like a lot of people were going to evacuate the town. I think they figured there was going to be a big battle in the town and they wanted out.

Every time we stopped, a few more trucks full of First Division soldiers would join our convoy. Finally I guess it was about 8:00 PM when we left town. We rode for about an hour or so, on this narrow paved two lane highway. Everything was okay, but a little later, we ran into mass confusion. Because coming down the road right at us, was an American convoy loaded with American soldiers. They almost ran us off the road. As we passed them they were all hollering to us, "You are going the wrong way." They said that the German tanks were coming, they were only about a mile away. We laughed and kept going. As we kept riding, we kept passing trucks and half-tracks all loaded with American soldiers, all retreating to the rear, away from the advancing German Army. After a while, we came upon American Infantry soldiers walking, trotting and running to the rear. I guess they ran out of vehicles and had to leave on foot. They kept telling us, "You are going the wrong way." They also said that the Germans were coming. Some of our guys hollered, "We are going the right way, you guys are going the wrong way. You are supposed to fight the Germans not run away from them." I didn't say anything, I just watched and listened as most of our guys did. After all, it was getting close to Christmas. "Tis the Season to be Jolly."

Well, after awhile there weren't any more retreating American soldiers, just the First Division riding along all by ourselves. After awhile, we stopped by a farm house. I guess this was our scheduled destination. Our Officers, who were leading the convoy in jeeps, went into the farmhouse. Then we looked around and saw a bunch of American Infantry soldiers all over the place. They weren't First Division soldiers, they were from a different division. At this time, I can't remember which division they were from. When our Officers were finished talking to their Officers, our Officers came out of the farmhouse and told us that we would probably stay here for the night, but not to disconnect the cannons from the half-tracks, just in case we had to move in a hurry. So we got off the half-tracks, and started to move around just to keep warm. There was about six inches of snow on the ground. After awhile, I told another Cannon Company soldier that I wanted a drink of water and he said he also wanted a drink of water, so we decided to go into the farmhouse for a drink of water. It was a big farmhouse; two stories high. The farmhouse was loaded with American soldiers, both Officers and Enlisted men. Some from the First Division and some from the other division. So we got a drink of water and decided to look around inside the farmhouse. After awhile, I said to the other soldier, "It's nice and warm in here." He agreed, so we looked around and found an empty space on the floor. We both laid down and went to sleep. We must have slept a few hours, then it became very noisy in the farmhouse. Somebody was yelling, "Everybody up, we are moving out." It was about

4:00 AM. So we got up and went outside and Cannon Company soldiers were mulling around the half-tracks.

At dawn, we mounted the half-tracks and continued up the same road. Every now and then we would stop for awhile and then move on. Around 8:00 AM we drove off the road and half way up a big hill. We were told we had a rush fire mission, so we unhooked the cannons from behind the half-tracks. In about five minutes the cannons were firing like mad. We must have fired for about twenty minutes. We then were told to dig the cannons in, and that we would stay here for awhile. Before the cannons were fully dug in, we got another fire mission. So the cannons immediately started firing, this time for about fifteen minutes. When it ceased firing, we continued digging the cannons in, and put up the camouflage nets over each cannon. Then we were told to dig fox holes, which we did. I only dug about two foot deep, because I thought we would be moving again. How wrong I was. We stayed there over two weeks. The next day, I dug my fox hole a lot deeper, and when I was done it was about five feet deep and about six feet long and about two and a half feet wide. Next I got a bunch of wood boxes that the 105mm shells came in, and filled them with dirt. Then I laid them across the top of my fox hole. I just left a little space at one end of the fox hole to crawl in and out of. I put two layers of dirt filled boxes on top of the fox hole. Then I put about two feet of dirt on top of the boxes.

When I got done, it looked like the kind of grave I used to see in the movies, where pioneers buried their dead on their way going out West, in the 1800's. I put a piece of wood over the opening so the snow, rain, or little animals couldn't get in. But it got so hot in there, I had to leave the piece of wood half off, otherwise I couldn't breath in there. At first, the walls and floor were all hard mud. The next night, the walls and floor became soft mud. So I got some more wood ammo boxes and put them on the floor, so I didn't have to sleep on the soft mud floor. The next night, due to condensation, ice started to form on the walls. I didn't knock it off, because it was better than mud. The ice kept getting thicker and thicker. But it wasn't too cold in there. I would say it was more hot than cold in there. The ice kept getting thicker and thicker. After awhile, I couldn't sleep on my back any longer. The ice got so thick I had to sleep on my side. I think every Cannon Company soldier had the same experience with icy walls in their fox holes.

About the second day at this location, we were high up on the same hill, when the Buzz Bombs started flying directly over the hill we were on. We weren't the target of the Buzz Bombs. I don't know what the Germans were shooting the Buzz Bombs at. But wherever they were shooting them, we seemed to be in the middle, between their launch pads and their targets.

I will now explain what a Buzz Bomb is. Actually it is a flying bomb with wings on it. They look like small airplanes. The bomb is a very big thing, probably a thousand pound bomb, maybe bigger. They have a motor on them. It is a rather noisy motor, so as long as the motor keeps running, everything is okay. While the motor keeps running, the Buzz Bomb just keeps flying by, like an airplane. But when you hear the motor stop, then it's a whole different story. When the motor stops, you might say the Buzz Bomb is out of gas, and down it comes. It doesn't just come straight down it sort of glides down like an airplane making a landing, but when you are near the top of a big hill, and these things keep flying overhead, sometimes they look like they are only about four or five hundred feet above the top of the hill. A few times we heard their motors stop. But most of them went a little past us before exploding. One day the motor stopped before it reached us. We saw it silently sailing towards us. But all of a sudden, it went into a nose dive and went straight down. It hit the ground and exploded before it reached us. I am glad my Guardian Angel knew how to maneuver that thing.

The reason we went right to this location that first night, we were told, was because not far from where we were set up, two roads cross. Also there was a bigAmerican ammunition dump there. And not too far away there was also a huge American gasoline storage area. For the German offensive to succeed, they desperately needed to capture both storage dumps. We also needed what was in both dumps, therefore, the Germans didn't want to blow up the dumps and we didn't want to blow up the dumps either. Our Rifle Companies were on one end of the ammunition dump. And the German Infantry was on the other end of the same ammunition dump. We kept shelling the far side of the dump so the Germans couldn't get near it. Also, the reason we stayed at that location was the crossroads. When the Germans tried to bring in supplies, Cannon Company and all available American artillery would blow the German trucks and tanks to hell. We had the crossroads under direct observation. That is why we were firing the cannons both day and night. Every time the Germans tried to use the two roads, they would get bopped. About the third day, our infantry captured both dumps. Then we had more ammo than we needed. After that, we could really shoot up a storm. If I remember correctly, Cannon Company only had one man killed on that hill, and that was a mistake. We were high up on the hill and our own artillery, with Long Toms, 155mm cannons were behind us. They were firing just over the top of the hill we were on, and one of their rounds fell short into our position. Our guy was killed instantly. I started to go towards him, with my first aid kit, but the Sergeant grabbed my arm and said, "Don't go, there is nothing left of him." So I didn't go. When we realized it was our own artillery that was shelling our position, we all jumped into our fox holes. And our Captain O'Brien got right on the field phone and ordered all American field artillery in the area to cease fire;

which they did. It is a good thing he did that. If he didn't do it, the Long Toms could have wiped out our whole Cannon Company.

The next day the clouds lifted, and the skies cleared. That's when our Air Force went to work. Our dive bombers just kept flying up and down all the roads, bombing and strafing the German tank convoys and truck convoys. Our Air Force had a field day. The German tanks were like sitting ducks on the roads. The day the clouds lifted, you might say the Germans were caught with their pants down. They had no place to go. No matter where they went, our dive bombers would bop them. The Germans never did reach their main objectives, the American main supply dumps in Antwerp and Brussels. A lot of the German tanks just ran out of gas, and had to be abandoned along the highways. When our Air Force got done with them, the Germans were surrendering in droves. I guess it could be compared to Napoleon's retreat from Russia, many years before. I guess world leaders will never learn, they should stay within their own boundaries, and make the most of what they have.

Around this time, we were told that those American soldiers who we passed on the road a few weeks ago, who were retreating the night we left the rest area to go back on line, at the beginning of the Battle of the Bulge. We were told they were a new outfit, just over from the States, and they were only on line a few days, when the Germans broke through their lines. We were also told they regrouped and went right back on line.

About the third week of January, 1945, at mail call, I received a beautiful letter from that very pretty Belgium lady. I read it over and over again. The Germans never did reach her town and she was all right. She asked me to send her a letter. But I decided not to. I figured she was a beautiful woman, and a beautiful person. I also figured she had a husband and a beautiful baby. She also had a beautiful home. I figured the best thing for her, was for me to drop out of her life, which I did. After all, before the war, I had a job in a Manhattan machine shop. My salary was about $18.00 a week. I also figured if I did survive the war, when I got back home, "Rosey, the Riveter" would have more experience as a machinist than me. So they would probably hire "Rosey the Riveter" instead of me. I grew up during the Depression, so when I got a job as a machinist for $18.00 a week, I felt like a millionaire. But in all reality, I knew I couldn't get married and raise a family on $18.00 a week. That's the reason I didn't answer her beautiful letter. That's about all I remember about the Battle of the Bulge.

CHAPTER TEN:

BACK TO GERMANY

After the Battle of the Bulge we worked our way back into Germany. We captured a few German towns, then we moved into the Hurtgen Forest.

For some reason, which I don't understand, I realize now that I have very little recollection of what happened in the Hurtgen Forest. I think we were in the forest for weeks, how many weeks we were in the forest, I can't remember. The only thing I clearly remember about the Hurtgen Forest, was a period of about a week, before we broke out of the forest. We were at this location at the East end of the forest and were there about a week. It was a very dangerous location for Cannon Company. We were set up and dug in very deeply. We were just a few feet into the forest under the outer row of trees. In front of us, was a very strange scene. There was nothing but flat open farmland. No trees, no hills, nothing but flat land as far as the eye can see. There were only a few small scattered farmhouses.

We were told not go out in the clearing, to stay out of sight under the trees in the forest so the Germans couldn't see us. We were told that the

German Infantry was dug in about three quarters of a mile in front of us. And behind them, German artillery and tanks were dug in and manned. We were told that the tanks may attack us at any time. If so, we would have to swap shots, direct fire with the tanks, just as Cannon Company had done the first few days in Sicily. We stayed at this particular location for about a week.

Then early one morning it happened as planned. We knew what was going to happen, we were told in advance. We were told there were a couple of other American Infantry Divisions besides the First Infantry Division, hiding in the Hurtgen Forest. Also hiding in the Hurtgen Forest, all Divisions also had their full artillery support such as mortar crews, anti-tank crews, Cannon Company crews, 105 mm artillery crews and 155 mm, Long Tom crews.

Then it happened on schedule, as planned. At a certain planned time, all at once, all the American artillery and mortar crews hiding in the forest started firing at the same time. We were all firing what is called a rolling barrage. What is meant by a rolling barrage is this. All the cannons and mortars start firing at the same time. Each starts firing as far out as it can. The whole thing is well planned. Each cannon or mortar fires to the right and left a few times then they decrease the distance a little and then fire to the right and to the left. They keep decreasing the distance and keep firing right and left. This went on for about forty five minutes maybe longer. We were told that extra artillery units were brought in for this operation. When we all started firing the sound was deafening. There must have been a few hundred cannons all firing at the same time. When it first started, the German artillery started firing back at us. But that didn't last long. They must have been knocked out within the first fifteen minutes. If I remember correctly, Cannon Company just stayed at this same location for another day, while the Rifle Companies pushed forward taking numerous prisoners.

After the Hurtgen Forest, things were going good for us, and we captured quite a few towns.

Then one day they told us that if we wanted to go to Mass, in a Catholic Church in one of the German towns we had captured, we could sign up to go. I think everybody in Cannon Company signed up to go to Church. I think for the same reason I signed up, so we could see what the German girls looked like. Being that almost all of Cannon Company signed up to go to Church they couldn't let everybody go. So they only let a few of us go. I was one of the lucky ones. We drove to Church in a half-track. It was a very big Church in a large town. The Church was in perfect shape. It had not been bombed or strafed. The Mass had started when I got there. There were half First Division Rifle Company soldiers and half civilians. The First Division soldiers had their rifles with them. I walked slowly down the center aisle, and was looking for some pretty German girls to sit next to. There were a lot of pretty girls, but the Rifle Company soldiers were sitting next to all the pretty girls. Finally, I spotted one very pretty girl, but she was with her elderly grandparents. So I sat in the pew in front of her. Whenever it was time to stand up, kneel down, or sit down. I would twist my head, so I could get a peek at her. I think I didn't pay too much attention to the Mass that day, but I think the good Lord knew why, after all, pretty girls were his idea. It was a nice and respectable congregation just like back home. When Mass ended, all the First Division soldiers sort of stepped aside and told the German girls to go ahead of them, I guess so they could get a better look.

But as I say, everyday is a new adventure. I remember in Germany one night, we set up the cannons in the dark. It was about a mile from where we were scheduled to cross the Roer River. Our Rifle Companies were on our side of the river, and the German Infantry was on the other side of the river. In the morning, they started shooting at each other, and we kept shooting the cannons over the river at the Germans.

Around noon time, we heard a whole bunch of big bombers coming at us, we looked up and saw they were our bombers. We all started waving and hollering, "Give em Hell fellows." We were at one end of a big wheat field, and at the other end of the wheat field was a fair size town, which we had taken the day before. While we were looking at the bombers, we thought they were going to start bombing the Germans, on the other side of the Roer River, but instead, when they got over the town, which we had taken the day before, they started dropping their bombs, and we were only about a quarter mile away and they were coming straight at us. There must have been about thirty or so bombers. When we saw what was happening we rolled out our signal carpets all over the ground. A signal carpet is about twenty feet long and about two feet wide. We have all different color signal carpets. Everyday we use as scheduled, or pre-planned a different color signal carpet. The idea of the signal carpets is to let the planes know that we are American soldiers, not to strafe or bomb us. The color that day was a bright yellow and it was a clear day. After they bombed the town, they just kept coming straight at us, and they just kept dropping bombs. I started saying prayers; I figured this is my last day on Earth. I didn't even hit the dirt. I figured no use, I am going to get killed and it didn't matter if I was standing or lying on the ground. So I just stood there and watched. The bombs just keep getting closer and closer. All of a sudden, the bombs stopped falling about two hundred yards before they reached us. We all figured they saw the yellow signal mats that we had rolled out on the ground. And we figured when they saw the signal mats, they stopped dropping bombs. We each thanked the Air Force boys, in our own way. We even drank a few toasts to them.

For over fifty years, from time to time, whenever I think of that day, I would thank the Lord for making the pilots see our yellow signal mats, and stop dropping the bombs.

But then about fifty years later, my wife and I were at a house party, up in Westchester County and I met this gentleman who turned out to have been an Army Air Force bomber pilot stationed in England during World War Two. We became friendly and we were discussing things that happened during World War Two. I happened to tell him how much I admired our Air Force during the war. I told him about the day they were dropping bombs, and when they saw our yellow signal mats, they stopped dropping their bombs about two hundred yards from our location. He told me, "I have news for you, once the bomb bay doors are opened, and the bombs start dropping, there is no way we can stop them from dropping." He said, "The only thing that saved you, was that the bombers ran out of bombs two hundred yards before they reached you." So he and I had a few more cocktails and changed the subject. I didn't like what he told me, but I did like the highballs. Then I figured my Guardian Angel worked a lot of overtime during the war, especially that day.

After the Roer River crossing, we fought through and captured various German towns on our way towards the Rhine River.

Our main objective at the Rhine River was the City of Bonn which had a big bridge crossing the Rhine River, which was still intact. We were hoping to capture the bridge intact, before the Germans had time to blow the bridge. But due to heavy resistance in Bonn, by the time the First Division reached the bridge, the Germans had blown the bridge. It took a few days to round up all the German prisoners in Bonn, because some of the German soldiers took off their uniforms and were wearing civilian clothes.

Therefore, it took about a week from the time the Ninth Armored Division captured and crossed the Remagen Bridge, before the First Infantry Division was able to cross the Remagen Bridge. Due to attacking, fighting and capturing the City of Bonn, I believe most of the First Infantry Division crossed the Rhine River on the Remagen Bridge before it finally collapsed. I guess due to artillery hits and the weight of our tanks continuously crossing, the old bridge just gave out. If the bridge could speak it would have probably said, "Enough is Enough."

But for some reason, Cannon Company didn't cross on the Remagen Bridge. We crossed on a pontoon bridge just South of the Remagen Bridge which First Army engineers built, in anticipation of the Remagen Bridge collapsing. I don't remember if the Remagen Bridge was still intact, or if it had already collapsed the day Cannon Company crossed the Rhine River on the pontoon bridge.

Well anyway, it went like this. Cannon Company was set up, not too far from the Remagen Bridge. Then early one morning we were told to pack up. We were moving out. About 5:00 AM we arrived at the pontoon bridge. Our Rifle Companies probably crossed over the pontoon bridge during the night. When we arrived at the pontoon bridge, it was empty and no one was on the bridge. We had half-tracks fully loaded and each half-track was pulling a cannon. We were told not to make any noise, but to drive the half-tracks out and onto the pontoon bridge, and we were told to keep about two hundred feet distance between each half-track and to drive very slowly. I was on about the third half-track and we drove up and onto the pontoon bridge. The water by the shore was very calm. The pontoon bridge was about three or four feet above the top of the water, but with the weight of the half-track on the pontoon bridge, we were now only about six inches above the top of the water. As we got about a third of the way out, there was a very strong current, and as a result of the current, the pontoon bridge seemed to have a slight curve to it. The weight of the half-track made it sort of a roller coaster ride. The bridge in front of us and behind us, was about three feet above the top of the water. But where the half-track was, the top of the bridge was only about six inches above the top of the water, and I never did like roller coasters. The bridge must have been at least a mile long. When I saw the strong currents and the pressure they were putting on the bridge and the weight of the half-tracks, plus the cannons making the bridge keep going up and down, I said to myself, "Now I know my mother will get that $10,000 from my GI insurance policy." We had a couple of guitars on the half-track which we picked up on our travels. There were a lot of Southern boys in Cannon Company, and they liked to sing songs and play the guitars. I could never sing, and in school the teacher made me a listener. I wasn't allowed to sing in school, but in the Army when we went out for a few drinks every now and then, if they were singing I would join in. Whenever I sang, they all laughed and as a result they nicknamed me "Gravel Gertie". Now we are on this pontoon bridge out in the middle of the Rhine River. I think everybody in Cannon Company was thinking what I was thinking; we will never make it across the Rhine River. We were all very quiet at that time, and nobody was talking. I guess just thinking and praying. When all of a sudden, one of the Cannon Company soldiers handed me a guitar and said, "How about a song Gravel?" Mind you, I am completely tone deaf and I don't know how to play any musical instrument, but I grabbed the guitar and sat at the top of the cannon ammunition and began to play the guitar and sing my two favorite songs: "It May be Nothing but a Shack" and "Down by the Railroad Tracks, but to Me It is

Home Sweet Home." Then I played and sang. "There'll be Blue Birds Over the White Cliffs of Dover. And there will be love and laughter and peace ever after and Johnny will come home to his own little room again, just you wait and see."

By the way, I never did learn the complete words of any song. Once I get started, I just sort of add my own words. When I got done, they were all laughing and clapping. The boys in the half-track in front and in back of us were also waving and laughing. Somebody from the half-track behind us hollered, "Sing it again Gravel." So I sang it again. By the time I got done singing, we were getting kind of close to the East side of the Rhine River and the water was calmer closer to the shore. At that point, we all knew we would make it across the Rhine River unless of course, the German artillery spotted us, which they didn't.

I wish I had written this book about forty years ago, when all these events were more vivid in my mind.

Many times, going through France and Germany, we were moving so fast and so far each day that we got shot at by our dive bombers and fighter planes. So many times we had to stop the half-tracks and roll out our signal carpets before our pilots would realize we were American soldiers. When they saw our signal carpets, they would stop bombing and strafing. Then they would fly by flapping their wings to let us know they got the message.

A very sad day in Cannon Company was the day our leader, Captain O'Brien of Cannon Company was killed. It was like losing a father. He was on the O.P. (Observation Post) directing and zeroing in our cannons firing at German infantry and tanks. I thought I would never forget exactly how he was killed, but at this time, I can't remember if he was killed by sniper fire or artillery fire.

But I do remember the day he was killed. First Lieutenant Golden was promoted to Captain and Second Lieutenant Ballard was promoted to First Lieutenant.

Promotions which they never wished for because they and every enlisted man in Cannon Company respected and admired Captain O'Brien. He was "First Division All The Way." "No Mission Too Difficult, No Sacrifice Too Great, Duty First." That was Captain O'Brien.

Then about a month or so later, Captain Golden was also killed on the O.P. He was killed by sniper fire. Then First Lieutenant Ballard became Captain of Cannon Company. Captain Ballard survived the war. Thank the Lord.

One day, a few weeks after we crossed the Rhine River, we were in a farming area. I don't remember what the name of the town was. We set the cannons up in a big wheat field. At the far end of the field was a big farmhouse. Some Cannon Company soldiers were in the big farmhouse.

All of a sudden, they called me and hollered for me to bring my medical kit. I thought somebody was hurt, so I ran as fast as I could. When I reached the farmhouse, I asked what the problem was. The soldiers outside the house pointed for me to go into the house, which I did. When I entered the house, all the soldiers started to laugh. I had no idea what was going on. All of a sudden two elderly women came into the room where I was, and a few of the soldiers pointed at me and told the two elderly women that I was a doctor. When they heard that, they both grabbed me and ushered me upstairs. I figured somebody upstairs must be wounded so I followed them. They went down a long hallway and opened a door at the end of the hallway. They went in, and I followed them. I found myself in a huge, nicely decorated bedroom. There was a huge bed in the center of the room. I still didn't know what was going on. As I approached the bed, I could see that there was somebody in the bed. As I got closer, I finally realized what the problem was. Lying on the bed was a very beautiful young German girl. Her tummy was puffed up like a balloon. It looked as if she was going to have a baby at any moment. I explained to her and the two elderly women that I was not a doctor, that I was a First Aid man for the soldiers and that I didn't know how to deliver a baby. They were all very sad, but they said they understood and they thanked me and the two elderly women said they would do it. When I went downstairs, all the soldiers were laughing and they asked if it was a boy or a girl.

One night we pulled into a small town. It was only about two blocks long. First we searched the houses, looking for German soldiers. There weren't any German soldiers, so we then set up the cannons and dug fox holes, and spent the night there. In the morning we could hear shooting in the distance, but not close enough to bother us. After awhile, we started walking around looking at the town. It was an odd sort of town, only about two blocks long and all the houses were on the same side of the street. We knew all the houses were occupied by civilians. Families were living in each house. We saw them the night before, when we were searching for German soldiers, but now it was about 10:00 AM and no civilians were out on the street. They must have been hiding in the houses. I guess they were afraid of us and were probably terrified and praying that we would not harm them. Every now and then we could see some of them peeking out of the windows at us. When we saw them looking out the windows, we would smile and wave at them. After awhile, a few of them would come out and sit on their front stoops, talking among themselves and watching us. When we walked by, we would smile and wave at them. After awhile, they realized they were safe, that we meant them no harm. Then awhile later, I guess they all came out. The stoops, sidewalk and street were loaded with civilians. Old men, old women, younger women pushing baby carriages and young children running around playing. It looked like a Sunday afternoon back in the States. That went on until about 3:00 PM. Then all of a sudden the Germans started shelling the town. I was with two Cannon Company soldiers in front of one of the houses when the shelling started. In about two minutes the streets were empty. An old lady was standing with her door open and waving for us to come into her house. We laughed and said, "Okay." When we entered the house, she motioned for us to follow, which we did. She went down into the cellar and we followed. When we got down there, they had kerosene lamps lit. It was a good size cellar and it was loaded with people. It was like an air raid shelter. She motioned for us to sit down, which we did. There were mostly old people and some young children. There were also two young women holding their babies. The shelling only lasted about fifteen minutes. None of the shells hit this house, but you could hear the shells hitting some of the other houses and exploding out in the street. We stayed there until the shelling stopped. While there, we were looking at them and they were looking at us. Nobody really talked and I think some of the old ladies were praying. While sitting there I was thinking how crazy war really is. Here we are, three American soldiers and all these German civilians. We are all hoping the same thing, that a shell wouldn't come crashing through the house and explode in the cellar. If it did, it would have probably killed all of us. Here we were sitting and all looking at each other. I was not a bit mad at them. As a matter of fact, I felt very sorry for them and I could tell they were not a bit mad at us. If anything, they were also feeling sorry for us. They were caught in a helpless situation and we were also caught in a helpless situation. When the shelling stopped, we all stood up to leave and we all shook hands and hugged each other, then we left. We went behind the houses where the cannons were set up. Everything was okay, nobody in Cannon Company got hit and no cannons or half-tracks were hit. We never did fire the cannons from that location. We left there early the next morning. As we were leaving, all the civilians came out and waved to us. We all waved back at them.

About a week later we pulled into this big beautiful valley. It was like a ranch or some sort of farm complex. There was a big beautiful house there. There were corrals and horse stables, then separated by quite a distance from the big beautiful house, were small barrack like buildings. I think they were fenced in. We set the cannons up high on a big hill overlooking the entire ranch complex. A few of our Rifle Companies were dug in around there also. We arrived there early in the morning and it was very quiet, no shooting. There were horses in the stables and also horses in the corrals. They were beautiful looking horses and looked well cared for. After awhile,

137

a few of the Rifle Company soldiers got permission from their Officers to ride the horses. After awhile, Cannon Company soldiers were also given permission by our Officers to ride the horses. There must have been about thirty horses there. At first, our guys rode the horses around in the corral, but after awhile, the Officers gave permission to open the corral and ride them all around the valley. Some of our guys were riding bare back, some were using saddles. After awhile, they started racing the horses up and down the hill and all over the valley. It looked like a rodeo. Some Cannon Company soldiers asked if I wanted to ride. I told them I knew how to ride a subway train but not a horse. Later that afternoon our Officers told them to put the horses back in the stables and corrals, which they did.

After awhile some men, women and children came out of the barrack-like buildings at the far end of the valley. They turned out to be Russian farm workers who were shipped here from Russia. There must have been about fifty of them. They asked if they could have one of the horses. Our Officers said, "Yes." They led one of the horses away from us. Next they killed and skinned the horse then they cut him up for food. I don't remember if they shot the horse or killed him some other way. One of them was like a butcher. He was cutting out horse steaks. It was like a big celebration. They were lined up waiting to get a piece of horse steak. One of the Russian women came over near us, and held up a piece of horse steak, and asked if we wanted it. We said, "No thanks." She said that it was good and walked away with her prize. I guess when you are hungry, you're hungry. When there was nothing left of the horse, they all went back into the compound. I guess they had a barbecue. I have a few pictures of some Cannon Company soldiers sitting around some of our dug in cannons up on the side of the hill, watching what went on that day. I think we left there the next day.

I often wonder what went on between the Russian farm workers and the German family who owned the valley, and lived in that big beautiful house after we left. After all, when we left, they were liberated, free to go and do whatever they wanted to do. I think the German family would have been smart to leave there, before we left. But I don't think they did.

War is a very unpredictable thing. One day you are a winner, the next day you are a loser. One day you have two legs, the next day you may not have any legs. One day you can see and everything looks beautiful. The next day you could be stumbling in the dark for the remainder of your miserable life. That is, if you can call it a life.

CHAPTER ELEVEN:

CZECHOSLOVAKIA

A few weeks before the war ended, we were chasing the retreating German army. We were riding on half-tracks, riding through one town after the other, then one Sunday afternoon a very funny thing happened. We drove through a large town and it was a beautiful town very neat and clean, not a bit marred by the war. We drove right through the center of town and there were beautiful shopping stores and sidewalk restaurants and cafes, on the left side of the street, was a beautiful well manicured park with beautiful fountains, and a very wide walkway running the length of the park. It was like a Sunday afternoon back home. Everybody was dressed in their finest Sunday garments. Families were walking along Main Street, ladies pushing their baby carriages, and small children walking along with them. Both sides of the street were loaded with people taking a leisurely Sunday afternoon stroll. The tables at the sidewalk cafes were all occupied. There were German soldiers and Officers strolling along with their wives and girlfriends. And here we were on our half-tracks, each half-track pulling a dirty old cannon. Each half-track was also carrying Rifle Company soldiers, besides we Cannon Company soldiers. There we are all dressed and ready for battle, and there they are all dressed and ready for partying. We were riding slowly through town, more or less taking in the sights. When the German soldiers and civilians realized we were American Infantry soldiers riding through their town, they were taken completely by surprise and didn't know what to do. So they just stood there looking and waving at us in a surprised and friendly manner. We smiled and waved back at them as we slowly rode through their beautiful town. We all had a big laugh as we left town and continued pursuing the retreating German Army.

We all agreed that what must have happened there was this, for about two weeks we had been moving very fast, covering a lot of miles chasing the retreating German Army. We were going through one town after another, like a bat out of a hell. Because of the way they were retreating, they probably had very little or no communication between Army Divisions. As a result, all the people including the German soldiers and Officers in the town we had just left, probably thought the front lines were about a hundred miles away, and they just couldn't believe it when they saw us riding through their town. I think we were in and out of their town before they realized what was actually taking place. The German soldiers and Officers we saw in that town didn't look like combat soldiers. They didn't have any weapons. Their uniforms and boots were all clean and shiny. They looked as though they were all on a weekend pass. We were moving so fast and far everyday, that I don't remember if that town was in Germany or Czechoslovakia.

Around that time another town we were riding through, just on the outskirts of town, there was a concentration camp. The German soldiers must have known we were coming and must have just left. The inmates in the concentration camp were still locked up inside a big barbed wire fence. They were looking at us and waving as we rode by. It was a very sad sight. They looked like walking skeletons. They looked very weak and sickly and we all felt very sad looking at them. They were waving at us to open the big barbed wire gate. But we didn't stop, we were still chasing the retreating German Army.

When our Officers saw what the situation was, I guess they contacted Division Headquarters who in turn probably contacted Core Headquarters who must have sent a fleet of Army doctors to care for them. Looking at them, it was obvious that they needed very special medical attention and very special diets, which only doctors could prescribe. As we proceeded onward, we came upon a second gate. This gate was open, and the inmates were starting to leave the concentration camp. I don't know if the inmates opened the gate or if our Rifle Company soldiers, who were standing around opened the gate. The right thing would have probably been to wait for doctors to check them and give them medication before releasing them. But it was such an unexpected situation. Nobody really knew what to do. So I guess everybody just acted on an impulse, and did what they thought was best for the prisoners. I know the prisoners were overjoyed to leave the prison. Who wouldn't be? But they had no place to go, no food, no clothes, all they had to wear was their dirty, filthy prison uniforms.

I do believe this was undoubtedly the saddest sight I have ever seen in my entire life. I have seen a lot of badly wounded and dead soldiers but all that happened quickly in battle.

These people were slowly being starved to death, and were constantly being humiliated and slowly being tortured both mentally and physically, for no reason whatsoever, they never committed any crimes.

How one human being could possible inflict such misery and suffering both physically and mentally on another human being is absolutely impossible for me to comprehend. To say it is absolutely disgusting is putting it much too mildly.

After seeing this horrible sight, it was then that I, for the first time, fully realized why this horrible war had to be fought.

Since the war ended, every now and then, in my spare time when I think about the war various thoughts enter my mind. One of the more frequent thoughts being what if Germany had won the war? Would Hitler continue killing Jews until there were none left on Earth? If so, what nationality would be next, the Irish then the Italians, and so on, and so on until the only nationality remaining on earth would be Germans? Would that have been Hitler's ultimate goal? A kind of scary thought isn't it?

When Germany Surrendered - May 8, 1945.

The cannons were set up near some small houses, but I don't remember the name of the town. It was in Czechoslovakia someplace. I think it was a bright sunny day, and around noon time we were told that Germany surrendered unconditionally. But we were also told that there could also be more fighting with the German Army. Because the German Army had been retreating on all fronts to regroup and have one last battle. Also, communications between various German Army Divisions was just about non-existing. There was mass confusion in what was left of the German Army. We were told, due to their lack of communication between various German Divisions, it is very possible that some German Divisions may not have known the war had ended. As a result, we could be attacked at any time. Therefore, we were told to act as though the war was still going on. We were told, if fired upon, to fire back. But only fire, if fired at. We were also told that some German outfits may know the war is over, but if they are fanatical enough, they may not surrender. They may continue fighting until they are killed. If so, we must accommodate them. Luck was on our side. For once we were told that the war was over, we never had to fire the cannons again. The German soldiers just kept surrendering. In a way, I felt sorry for them. They were going home to bombed out cities, towns and villages. Most of the German towns were nothing but piles of rubble with no drinking water, no gas or electric. I think Adolph took the easy way out.

When it became obvious that there weren't going to be any more battles, Cannon Company was pulled off line, or out of the woods, or fields, or whatever you want to call it. And we moved into a fairly large town in Czechoslovakia. Our kitchen was set up in sort of a big courtyard where there were large wooden tables and benches. First we would line up, and go past a long table full of big pots of food. The cooks would load our mess kits with food. Then we would sit at the tables and eat our food. It was sort of an open courtyard. At the far end of the courtyard, next to the entrance or exit of the courtyard, our cooks set up a few large new galvanized garbage cans. After we finished eating, any food that we had left over, which we didn't eat we would dump into the garbage cans. Then we would wash and rinse our mess kits. There was a very sad sight outside the courtyard. Standing on the sidewalk and street, were a bunch of old ladies, old men, young women and children. They were carrying pots and large metal dippers. When we were all finished eating, they were allowed into the courtyard. It was very sad to watch them digging into the garbage cans for scraps of food. They were very orderly, no pushing or shoving. They would each take a pot full of scraps and leave. After a day or so, we all had girlfriends. They didn't have to go to the garbage cans for food. It was a very funny sight, all Cannon Company soldiers who had girlfriends, when finished eating, would go back on line and get seconds. Next, all you would see was Cannon Company soldiers walking through town carrying an open mess kit, full of food and a canteen cup full of coffee. I had to carry a canteen cup full of milk, because my girlfriend had a small baby. Our mess Sergeant said he had to order a lot of extra food, and it was a lot of extra work cooking the food, but the cooks didn't mind, because they also had girlfriends who needed food. We stayed there about a week or so, and it was a very sad day for us and the civilians when we were told we had to pack up and leave. I know, if we took a vote, all Cannon Company would have voted to stay there for an extended period of time. But soldiers don't vote, they just obey orders. Then we moved to a few other small towns around there.

After awhile, being that the war was over, all the medics were called together as a group. We ended up in a fairly good size town in Czechoslovakia called Francensbad. It was a beautiful neat and clean town, no war damage that I could see. The medics all moved into a large hotel in the best part of town. We were told that the town of Francensbad was a very famous town before the war. Wealthy people from all over the world came there. It was known for some sort of health spas. We stayed in the hotel for about two weeks, and had a First Aid station set up someplace on the first floor for the First Division soldiers. Our officers also allowed civilians who needed first aid, to come into our aid station. One evening while I was on duty in the aid station, a very pretty blond haired lady brought her young son, about six years old into the Aid Station. I forgot what his problem was. I think he had a sore throat. She was very friendly, and we sat and talked for awhile. She told me she was an opera singer before the war. I looked at my watch and told her that it was getting near curfew time. When she realized how late it was, she became very excited because we both knew the curfew was for soldiers and civilians. I think the curfew started about 8:30 PM. We both knew that the curfew was strictly enforced and at 8:30 PM sharp, a bunch of First Division MP's would cruise around town in two and a half ton trucks. No matter who they found outside of a building they would put violators on the two and half ton trucks and lock them up for the night. It didn't matter if it was a First Division soldier or a civilian. If you were found outside, you were locked up. When I told her what time it was, she became terrified and asked if I would walk her home. I said, "Okay," so we left the aid station. She was walking so fast, I practically had to trot to keep up. She was holding her son's hand and kept telling him to hurry. Every time she looked at her watch, she would go faster. We kept going and going and going. I kept asking where she lived. She kept saying a little further, a little further, every time I asked. We kept going in and out of different streets. Finally I looked at my watch and told her, I had to go back. She said just a little further, so I followed. Finally I said, "It's too late, I must go back." So I turned around and left. About half way back, I saw the MP trucks coming. There were apartment houses there, and I saw a lady looking out the first floor window. She pointed to the MP trucks and said, "MP". She knew they would lock me up if they saw me. So I asked her if I could come into her apartment. She laughed and said, "Okay." So I spent the night there. I never did see the opera singer again.

A day or so later, we were all asked if we wanted to remain in the Army and make a career of it, or if we wanted to be sent back to the States and discharged to become civilians. At that time, I had attained the rank of T-3. Now I had to make a very important decision; to either stay in the Army or become a civilian. So I pondered the problem and figured that if I became a civilian, it would be very difficult to find a job, because thousands and thousands of discharged soldiers, sailors, and Marines would be out looking for jobs every day, and not enough jobs to go around. After all, the war was over, and all the factories that were producing war material, such as tanks, guns, airplanes, medical supplies, uniforms and such were all going out of business, and closing down. Thousands of people from all these factories were now being laid off.

So I figured between the discharged soldiers, sailors, and Marines and unemployed defense workers it would be very difficult to find a decent job. Then I figured if I remained in the Army, I would probably die in an Army alcoholic ward in about three years. So I decided to become a civilian. We were told that if we became civilians, and didn't like it, and if we re-enlisted within six months, we could come back into the Army with the same rank that we held when we were discharged. So I figured that if I came back into the Army again, I would still be a T3, and that's not too bad. So I told them I would become a civilian. I figured if I couldn't find a decent job within five months, I would probably go back into the Army.

After about two weeks in Francensbad, a bunch of us who decided to leave the Army were put on trucks and sent to various other Divisions who hadn't seen too much combat in Europe. After Germany surrendered, we were still at war with Japan. That's the reason we were sent to those other Divisions. They were scheduled to be sent back to the States, and from there, they were scheduled to be sent to the Pacific theater of operations to fight the Japanese Army. The First Division was scheduled to stay in Germany as an occupational Army to maintain the peace. Therefore, we were just put into these other various divisions as passengers to get a ship back to the States. I was sent to the town of Elboken in Czechoslovakia. I believe I joined the 99th Division for the trip home. They were a very friendly group. I have a picture of myself and a few of them outside a store in Elboken that we used as a First Aid Station. I stayed there for about two weeks, and then sent to a different outfit. Finally I ended up in Le Havre, France to wait for a ship to take us back to the States. While waiting in an Army tent city near Le Havre I was able to get a one day pass to visit Paris. We arrived in Paris about noon, by a small truck convoy. Two other soldiers and I decided to go touring together. First we had lunch at a sidewalk cafe, then we walked around and saw the Eiffel Tower. We just looked at it but didn't go into it. Then we went down some steps and walked along the River Seine. It was a fancy place and I knew it was a famous tourist attraction, because I had seen it in the movies and magazines at various times. Then we went to a few more sidewalk cafes, had a few drinks and watched the girls go by. Before we knew it, it was time to get on the trucks and go back to camp. I figured I had to visit Paris, or my European tour wouldn't have been complete.

A day or so later, we boarded a Troop ship which took us to Boston. I stayed in Fort Miles Standish near Boston for about a week. The first night there, I went to the PX and had ice cream, but I hadn't had ice cream for about three years, and I ate so much of it, that I ended up with a stomachache.

We left Fort Miles Standish by train, which took us to Fort Dix in New Jersey and I stayed there about a week. And then I was discharged from the United States Army, with an Honorable Discharge on October 21, 1945.

CHAPTER TWELVE:

HEY MOM, I MADE IT

Now I was on my own. No more free food. No more free clothing. No more free transportation. No more all-expense paid vacations. "The End," or should I say the "Beginning." Now the scary part, I had to find a job.

So I became a civilian, and went home to Bayside West, Long Island, New York.

My mother, father and sister Grace were very glad to see me and I was happy to be home.

My two older brothers were still in the service. Brother Jerome in the Sea Bees and brother John in the Air Force.

I did a lot of partying mostly in the local taverns. Every now and then I would stop partying and go look for a job. After about four months of partying and looking for a job, and not finding a decent job, I told my mother that I was thinking about going back into the Army. Every time I mentioned it, she would start crying and begging me not to go back into the

Army. As a result of the way my mother acted, I never did go back into the Army.

But I shall never forget those years during the War, which certainly prepared me for whatever life would hold for me in the future.Note - The names of certain people have been changed, so as not to offend anyone. They were all very brave and very good soldiers who were all very good friends of mine. The story was written to present the facts the way I remember them.

George A. Flynn

George A. Flynn

As far as the following pictures are concerned, you must realize that when things are going bad for us, and we are being heavily shelled by the enemy, nobody is walking around taking pictures.

The only time the cameras come out, is when everything is going good for us, and nobody is shooting at us. I know the pictures look like we are on a Sunday picnic, but it wasn't really like that.

George A. Flynn

This is a picture of me, the author. The picture of me sitting on the motorcycle was taken during the War someplace on the East side of the Rhine River in Germany. This is a German Army motorcycle which was picked up on our travels. Our guys painted a white star in a white circle on the front side and rear of the motorcycle, so that the rifle company soldiers would know that the motorcycle is now an American motorcycle. That way our guys could ride around without getting shot at by our own troops.

The bottle of booze and the top hat were also prizes of War taken from the house to my right. To my left, about two hundred feet away, not shown in this picture, the cannons are all set up and firing.

This is a picture of me, the author, taken during the War, someplace in Germany. The cannons are set up and firing to my left. The belt I am wearing, I picked up during the Sicilian campaign. I can't remember if it is a German soldier's belt or an Italian soldier's belt. The trinkets on the belt I picked up at various times. I can't remember if they are from a German or Italian soldier's uniform. After a while in Germany, I decided to throw the belt away. I decided if I was ever taken prisoner, my captors wouldn't think too kindly of me wearing their belt and trinkets.

This a picture of some of our Cannon Company soldiers. The fourth soldier from the left is Staff Sgt. Biff Grimes. The picture was taken during the War in Germany, just outside of Aachen. Sgt. Biff Grimes survived the War. If memory serves me correctly, all soldiers in this picture survived the War.

After the War ended, we all went our separate ways. What I am hoping is that Biff Grimes reads this book. I would like to have a chat with him, and ask him what happened to me on D-day Normandy, France when he came down the hill about noon time and told us to follow him up the hill. I remember standing up and getting ready to follow him up the hill. The next thing I remember it's dark and I am digging a fox hole on top of the hill.

George A. Flynn

This picture was taken during the War in Germany, near Aachen. We are from left to right, me the author, a German soldier, but we didn't know he was a German soldier at the time the picture was taken. Next is Stewart West, far right is Sgt. Mutter. We stayed at this location for about two weeks, firing the cannons both day and night. The day we were leaving this location, the German soldier put on his uniform, came out of his house and surrendered.

This picture was taken during the War, someplace in Germany. The cannon is dug in, set up and ready for fire again. The soldier on the left is Staff Sgt. Kroleski. He was a regular Army career soldier. He had about 12 years in the Army when this picture was taken. He went overseas with the First Division. He fought through all eight major campaigns with the First Division. He survived the War. I can't remember the names of the other soldiers in this picture. Off to the right and rear of the cannon, can be seen a pile of spent cartridges.

George A. Flynn

This is a picture of one of the cannons, set up and ready for fire, but not fully dug in. This picture was taken in Germany on a slow day. We did very little firing from this location. This is overlooking the valley where our guys were riding horses. I am on the right.

162

This is a picture of Cpl. Pluggy Kluze, which was taken during the War, somewhere in Germany. The cannons are dug in down the hill in front of Pluggy Kluze. There was a lull in the firing that day. Somebody found a camera and went around taking pictures. Pluggy Kluze was on the same Duck, on D-day Normandy France as myself. He was the last soldier to jump off the Duck just before it sank about eight miles out. He was the last one to see Pvt. Leonard, who went down with the sinking Duck. Pluggy was wounded in one of the battles in France, evacuated to the hospital, recovered and rejoined Cannon Company. He survived the War.

This picture is of Cpl. Pluggy Kluze and myself. It was taken during the War on a quiet day in Germany. The cannons are set up, about three hundred feet in front of us down the hill. This is the day our soldiers were riding the horses all over the valley. We are just sitting there, watching the rodeo.

This picture was taken in Germany during the War. It was a quiet day. The cannons are set up down the hill from where this picture was taken, being that there was no shooting that day. When the local civilians realized that we meant them no harm, some of them came out walking over near us. After awhile, one of our guys started taking pictures. In the front row is Sgt. Dutch Nestor sitting and talking to a pretty German girl. Dutch Nester had the edge on the rest of us in that he could speak perfect German. Standing to the right rear is Cpl. Pluggy Kluze. Sitting behind Dutch Nestor and the German girl is another Cannon Company soldier, talking to another pretty German girl. I can't remember that soldier's name. Sgt. Nestor fought through all eight campaigns. He also survived the War.

This picture was taken in Czechoslovakia, about a week or two after the War ended. Sgt. Dutch Nestor on the left, and me, the author, on the right.

The cannon must think we are mad at it, because it hasn't been fired for about a week or two. That is most unusual for Cannon Company cannons.

About the Author

He was a soldier during World War II. He saw action in two continents –Africa and Europe. he made two D-Day invasions. He saw action in seven major campaigns.

Printed in the United States
96591LV00004B/252/A

9 781403 395016